The Christy Moore Songbook

Edited by Frank Connolly
Introduction by Donal Lunny

BRANDON

This collection first published 1984 by Brandon Book Publishers Ltd,
Cooleen, Dingle, Co. Kerry, Ireland;
and 51 Washington Street, Dover, New Hampshire 03820, U.S.A.

British Library Cataloguing in Publication Data
Moore, Christy
Songbook.
1. Folk songs, English
I. Title II. Connolly, Frank
784.4'942 M1738

ISBN 0-86322-063-0

Acknowledgements: to the Mechanical Copyright Protection Society and the
companies and individuals listed in the Index for permission to reproduce the songs.
Copyright in songs remains with authors.

Photo credits: Academy Press (115), Fergus Bourke (31;64), Cyril Byrne (16;61),
Colm Henry (6;9;11;53;113;131), Ann Egan (69),
Eamonn O'Dwyer (42;75;87;96;109), Art O'Laoghaire (123), Derek Speirs
(cover;111;139)

Cover design: Brendan Foreman and Flying Colours
Typesetting: Printset & Design Ltd, Dublin.
Printed and bound by Mount Salus Press Ltd, Dublin, Ireland.

Introduction

Donal Lunny, 1978. Colm Henry

Introduction

From the days when he was an irrepressible pupil giving his teachers grey hairs, Christy Moore was a singer. Sessions of music and song were frequent in his family — his mother Nancy loved and still loves creating opportunities for people to sing and play. Thus encouraged, albeit initially in a more genteel direction, Christy flourished and took his ability for granted in a comfortable way.

While he was still in Newbridge, Christy and I formed a rather short-lived duo called the Rakes of Kildare. It was on a casual basis — my brother Frank played whistle with us occasionally; yet at that time Christy was picking out songs: some from old books, some from the singing of people he met at sessions. Many of these later became favourites all over the country, whether sung by him or not. Two songs in particular come to mind: "Mary of Dungloe", which used to be in a waltz tune but which Christy changed to $\frac{4}{4}$ which is how it is best known; and "The Curragh of Kildare", for which he devised the chorus now used by anyone who sings it.

His first job on leaving school was as a bank clerk and he was shuttled furiously around the country, staying several months in each place. Clonmel, Askeaton, Ballyhaunis, Tulla and Milltown Malbay were among the towns in which he worked and these varied locales presented him with many opportunities to meet singers and musicians and to widen the scope of his collecting.

During the long bank strike in 1966, Christy left for England where he stayed for the next five years. He performed constantly in folk clubs round England and Scotland and came in contact with many Irish singers and musicians living and playing there. Among the most important of these were the Grehan sisters, who eventually led Christy to John Reilly in their home town of Boyle, Co. Roscommon. John gave Christy some of his finest traditional ballads, including "The Well Below the Valley", versions of which could be found in many other countries but which was hitherto unrecorded in Ireland or England. Christy also became friends with two of London's best loved Irish musicians, Liam Farrell and Raymond Roland.

On Christy's return to Ireland in 1971, he immediately organised and recorded the album, *Prosperous*. The effect of this album is still reverberating through Irish music today. The two most important songs on it were "The Raggle Taggle Gypsy" and "The Cliffs of Dooneen". Christy had the idea of leading directly from "The Raggle Taggle Gypsy" into an air called "Tabhair dom do Lámh". This, along with the prominence of the uileann pipes on the arrangement of "The Cliffs of Dooneen" brought traditional music to the attention of Irish people in a completely different way. Planxty, which formed directly after the recording of the *Prosperous* album, continued to combine songs and tunes in this manner and was a major factor in raising traditional music in people's consciousness.

This group was a great environment for the talents of all concerned. There was considerable variety in the scope of Christy's and Andy Irvine's songs, and Liam O'Flynn's piping received the respect and importance it deserved. My interest in arrangement was constantly being challenged by the discipline of traditional modes and how to get the most out of our instrumentation. It was a period of exploration and discovery, during which areas of Irish music previously considered remote were made accessible to a great number of listeners.

Wide though the range of Planxty was, many ideas and possibilities were coming up which could not be realised in that context. I left first, to learn about and play contemporary music. Christy left not long afterwards, one of the main reasons for his departure being the desire to sing songs which directly reflected his opinions on life and society. The solo albums which he recorded over the following three years contained many songs which would have sounded incongruous coming from Planxty, which had ultimately evolved into a form that would not embrace a sudden influx of different influences. These albums — *Whatever Tickles Your Fancy*, *Christy Moore*, *The Iron Behind The Velvet* and *Live in Dublin* — covered a wild variety of styles, from "The Limerick Rake", with two African drummers, to "Van Diemen's Land", with Robbie Brennan (drums), Jimmy Faulkner (electric guitar), Declan McNelis (bass) and Kevin Burke (fiddle).

Christy was responsible for the re-formation of Planxty in 1979. The Bothy Band, with which I had been playing, had just wound up, and he noticed that Andy and Liam were also available. So, with the addition of Matt Molloy, Planxty sailed once again. More musicians were subsequently involved from time to time, namely Noel Hill, Tony Linnane, Nollaig Ní Cathasaig and Bill Whelan. It was a good move on Christy's part, as he had in the intervening years accumulated many songs which were ideal Planxty material, such as "Little Musgrave", "The Ballad of Farmer Michael Hayes" (practically reconstructed by Christy) and "Lord Baker".

However, both Christy and I felt the need to move on. For some time I had been feeling the urge to create an effective link between Irish traditional music and the world of contemporary music (rock, disco etc.), mainly through the addition of bass and percussion. This concept was too radical for Planxty. Christy's eventual interest in this idea led to the formation of Moving Hearts. The initial direcon of this band was largely determined by Christy, who had a backlog of songs he had been gathering while with the re-formed Planxty.

Donal Lunny, Andy Irvine, the late Pat Dowling, Christy Moore, Liam Óg Ó Floinn, in Dowling's of Prosperous. Colm Henry

Beginning with Christy, Declan Sinnott and myself (a trio reassembled with great effect for the recent *Ride On* album) we rapidly expanded. Soon we became a powerful unit, adding conviction and credibility to whatever sentiment we chose to sing about. Songs like "No Time for Love" by Jack Warshaw and Jim Page's "Hiroshima Nagasaki Russian Roulette" were instantly popular. Many others gradually gained massive acceptance, such as "Irish Ways and Irish Laws" by John Gibbs and "What Will You Do About Me?". Christy very effectively adjusted Jessie O. Farrow's words to apply more accurately to Ireland. "On the Blanket" was probably the most direct statement made by the band. Written by and later jointly recorded with Mick Hanly, this song confronted people with the nightmare of H-Block and its surrounding political neuroses. The song was right for that moment and needed to be sung.

Nevertheless, Christy gradually realised that although the band was a formidable vehicle for his songs, it didn't suit him in several ways. He found himself having to sing differently to suit the band's music. The arrangements were complex and required much rehearsal. Altogether the band was taking up more of his life than he was comfortable with. The parting of ways was inevitable. But two albums had been recorded which had several great songs that have become part of the popular repertoire and will be sung for many years. Moving Hearts was crucial to Christy's progress, because it placed him before the public in a new, exciting way. It broke the mould of the balladeer with the guitar, enabling him to reach many people outside his normal audience. When he resumed his solo career, his following had increased yet again.

The next album, *The Time Has Come*, was in a way a reorientation, a necessary process of re-establishing his identity as a solo performer. This explains the re-recording of songs already on Planxty and Moving Hearts albums: "Faithful Departed", "All I Remember", "The Lakes of Ponchartrain" and "Only Our Rivers Run Free". This album also marks his emergence as a songwriter, with "The Wicklow Boy" and the title track, "The Time Has Come".

Christy's sense of immediacy had returned along with the relative simplicity of his performance. A good example of this immediacy was at a concert in UCD when, ten minutes before going on stage, he completed a satirical ballad about the Literary and Historical Society, which had behaved in an unworthy manner towards Danny Morrison the previous night.

Christy's songs span many aspects of life and living, more so than those of most singers. Some of the songs in this collection are just what they appear to be: good humoured nonsense. Contrasted with some of the great sweeping classic ballads like "Lord Baker" or "Little Musgrave" they cover a great range of emotional expression. What binds them together is Christy himself. The traditional ballads encompass a love of the country and its music. Many of the more recent songs speak of the ills of the country, the exploitation of people, the supression of minorities, the persecution of certain individuals because of their political beliefs. Many of the songs question the freedom of the individual in society, but the element which glimmers through all the way is a sense of justice. Justice in terms of how those with power behave towards those who are at their mercy, whether it be between one country and another, a giant multinational company and someone who gets in the way of 'progress', or a policeman and a traveller.

It is this sense of fair play that comes through and reaches the hearts of all people of goodwill, whether the principle is expressed as a cry of outrage or suffused in a welter of good humour. For many people the singing of these songs is a reassurance, an affirmation that others are aware of and wish to change what is going on in the world around them.

Donal Lunny
June 1984.

Moving Hearts. Colm Henry

9

Editor's Preface

Christy Moore and the musicians with whom he has played have made a major contribution to the development of Irish music over the last twenty years. Old songs have been resurrected and re-arranged and a music with strong roots in the past has emerged, full of ideas of the present and future, to renew a living tradition.

The rebirth of popular interest in traditional music has coincided with a reawakening of interest in Irish history and arts. Many musicians have involved themselves in progressive political struggles, writing and singing songs about current events and situations. Censorship of the national broadcasting service has prevented some of these songs from achieving wide circulation. In the six counties of Northern Ireland the renewal of traditional music has been particularly associated with the movement for national independence and freedom, and recent songs from Northern songwriters are included in this collection.

I hope that this book will help to increase familiarity with these songs, the majority of which have been recorded by Christy over the years. An index is included to direct readers towards the relevant recordings. It has not always been easy to decide which version of a song to publish here: Christy picks up songs and makes them his own, giving them a twist here and there, sometimes dropping verses, sometimes adding. He is always thinking about the songs and always developing, and the versions presented here are not necessarily the original or traditional versions; also, some are given as he performs them now rather than as he recorded them. Unfortunately, it has not been possible to get permission to include a few of the songs I had originally selected.

Thanks are due to — amongst others — Donal Lunny, for resting his bouzouki to pick up the pen and write the introduction; Des Moore, for writing the music; Cepta Hopkins, for typing the original draft of the manuscript; and the photographers.

Frank Connolly
August 1984

The Songs

I first heard it in Pat Dowling's in Prosperous sung by the Grehan sisters from Boyle, Co. Roscommon, who gave me my first break in the folk scene by allowing me to do support to them in Manchester around 1967. The song originated from the repertoire of the late John Reilly.

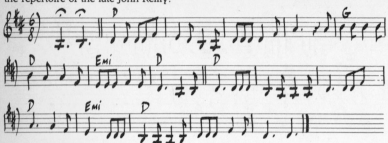

Oh there been a woman in our town, a woman you ought know well;
She dearly loved her husband and another man twice as well.

Chorus
With me right Finnickineerio, me tip finnick a wall,
With me right Finnickineerio,
We're tipping it up to Nancy.

She went down to the chemist shop some remedies for to buy:
'Have you anything in your chemist shop to make me old man blind?'

Chorus

'Give him eggs and marrowbones and make him suck them all.
Before he has the last one sucked, he won't see you at all.'

Chorus

She gave him eggs and marrowbones and made him suck them all.
Before he had the last one sucked, he couldn't see her at all.

Chorus

'If in this world I cannot see, here I cannot stay.
I'd rather go and drown myself.' 'Come on,' says she, 'and I'll show you the way.'

Chorus

She led him to the river, she led him to the brim;
But sly enough of Martin, it was him that shoved her in.

Chorus

She swam through the river, she swam through the brine.
'Oh Martin, dear Martin don't leave me behind.'
'Yerra shut up outa that ye silly aul fool'
'Ye know poor Martin is blind.'

Chorus

There's nine in me family and none of them is my own.
I wish that each and every man would come and claim his own.

Chorus

Avondale

I first heard it from Dominic Behan when he and I shared a stage in Shepherd's Bush in 1967; afterwards he amazed me with the extent of his repertoire, singing non-stop for two nights and a day with occasional breaks to go to the off-licence.

Chorus
Oh have you been to Avondale
Or lingered in her lovely vale
Where tall trees whisper all low the tale
Of Avondale's proud eagle?

Long years that green and lovely glade
Has nursed Parnell, her proudest Gael,
And cursed the land that had betrayed
Great Avondale's proud eagle.

Where proud and ancient glories fade,
Such was the place where he was laid.
Like Christ, was thirty pieces paid
For Avondale's proud eagle.

Chorus

The Sheriff and Gardaí supervise the eviction of Anne Fleming and other workers and their families from Ranks Mills in Dublin after an 18 month occupation. May 1984. Cyril Byrne.

Written by Donagh MacDonagh, I learned it in Glasgow in about 1966 from Arthur Johnston. It was with this song I made my debut on RTE in 1967.

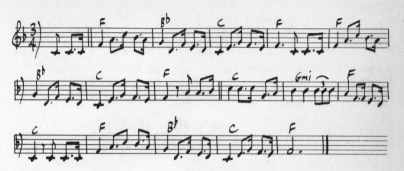

In Dublin city in 1913
The boss was rich and the poor were
    slaves,
The women working and the children
    hungry,
Then on came Larkin like a wave.

The workman cringed when the bossman
    thundered.
Seventy hours was his weekly chore.
He asked for little and less was granted,
Lest gettin' little he'd ask for more.

But on came Larkin in 1913,
A mighty man with a mighty tongue,
The voice of labour, the voice of justice,
And he was gifted and he was young.

God sent Larkin in 1913,
A labour man with a union tongue.
He raised the workers and gave them
    courage;
He was their hero, the workers' son.

It was in August the bossman told us
No union man for him could work.
We stood by Larkin and told the bossman
We'd fight or die, but we would not shirk.

Eight months we fought and eight months
    we starved.
We stood by Larkin through thick and
    thin,
But foodless homes and the crying
    children
They broke our hearts; we could not win.

When Larkin left us we seemed defeated.
The night was black for the working man,
But on came Connolly with new hope
    and counsel.
His motto was that we'd rise again.

In 1916 in Dublin city,
The English soldiers they burnt our town.
They shelled the buildings, and shot our
    leaders;
The harp was buried beneath the crown.

They shot McDermott and Pearse and
    Plunkett;
They shot McDonagh and Clarke the
    brave.
From bleak Kilmainham they took their
    bodies
To Arbour Hill to a quicklime grave.

But last of all of the seven leaders
I sing the praise of James Connolly,
The voice of labour, the voice of justice,
Who gave his life that men might be free.

As far as I can recall I wrote two verses of this version myself and the origins of the first two verses have disappeared into the mists of time.

As I went out by Dublin city
At the hour of twelve at night,
Who should I see but a Spanish lady
Washing her feet by candlelight.
First she washed them then she dried them all by the fire of the amber coal.
In all my life I ne'er did see a maid so sweet about the sole.

Chorus
Whack fal de to ra loo ra laddy,
Whack fal de to ra loo ra lay.

Oh I asked her would she come out walking
And we went on till the grey cocks crew.
A coach I stopped then to instate her;
We went on till the sky was blue.
Combs of amber in her hair and her eyes knew every spell.
In all my life I ne'er could see a maid whom I could love so well.

Chorus

Oh but when I came to where I found her
And set her down from the halted coach,
Who was there with his arms folded
But the fearful swordsman Tiger Roche.
Blades were out, 'twas thrust and cut and never the man gave me more fright
Till I laid him out upon the floor where she stood holding the candlelight.

Chorus

Oh so if you go to Dublin city
At the hour of twelve at night,
Beware o' young girls who sit in their windows
Washing their feet by candlelight.
I met one and we went walking; I thought that she would be me wife.
When I came to where I found her, if it wasn't for me sword I'd a lost me life.

Chorus

The Belfast Brigade

I suspect that I learned this song at a republican ballad session in Shepherd's Bush in 1966. In those days it was considered good fun to hear Paddy sing a rebel song; eighteen years later it could get you seven days at Her Majesty's pleasure.

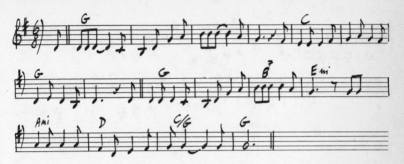

The Black and Tans from London came to shoot the people down.
They thought the IRA was dead in dear old Belfast town.
These cruel English gunmen they were seriously dismayed;
'No surrender' is the war cry of the Belfast Brigade.

Chorus
Glory Glory to old Ireland,
Glory Glory to us Ireland,
In glory to the memory of the men who found a grave;
'No surrender' is the war cry of the Belfast Brigade.

Chorus

They bombed us in the Shankill and way out in Antrim's glens.
They bombed us in the Falls Road and we bombed them back again.
They fired their long range cannons and we threw our hand grenades;
'No surrender' is the war cry of the Belfast Brigade.

Chorus

Oh we fought and beat the Black and Tans, we beat their every man,
Although we'd little in our hands, oh still they turned and ran.
We're out for our Republic and to hell with their Free State;
'No surrender' is the war cry of the Belfast Brigade.

Chorus

Written by Robbie Burns, the Scottish poet, and arranged into this particular
version by Donal Lunny and myself about 1962. The sorrow of a Glasgow woman
whose man is soldiering on the Curragh; she contemplates disguise and enlistment.

The winter it is past, and the summer's come at last
And the birds they are singing in the trees.
Their little hearts are glad but mine is very sad
For my true love is far away from me.

The rose upon the briar by the water running free
Gives joy to the linnet and the bee.
Their little hearts are blessed but mine it's not at rest
For my true love is absent from me.

A livery I'll wear and I'll comb back my hair,
In velvet so green I will appear.

Chorus
And it's straight I will repair
To the Curragh of Kildare
For it's there I'll find tidings
Of my dear.

All you that are in love and cannot it remove,
I pity the pain that you endure,
For experience lets me know that your hearts are full of woe
And a woe that no mortal can endure.

Chorus

This came via Andy Irvine from the singing of Maddy Prior, lead singer with Steeleye Span.

There were three drunken maidens
Came from the Isle of Wight.
They started to drink on a Monday,
Never stopped till Saturday night.

But when Saturday night it came, me
   lads,
Oh still they wouldn't get out
These three drunken maidens,
They pushed the jug about.

Then in came dancing Sally
With her cheeks as red as the bloom,
Saying, 'Move over me, jolly sisters,
And give young Sally some room.

'And I will be your equal
Before the evening's out.
And these three drunken maidens
They pushed the jug about.

They had woodcock and pheasant,
They had partridge and pear,
And every kind of dainty
No shortage there was there.

They had forty casks of beer, me lads,
Still they wouldn't get out.
These three drunken maidens
They pushed the jug about.

Then in came the landlord
He was looking for his pay
And the forty pounds bill, me lads,
These girls were forced to pay.

They had ten pounds a piece, me lads,
But still they wouldn't get out.
These three drunken maidens
They pushed the jug about.

'Where are your feathered caps,
Your mantles rich and fine?'
'They're all been swallowed up, me lads,
In tankards of fine wine.'

'And where are your fancy men,
Young maidens brisk and gay?'
'We left them in the ale-house
And it's there they'll have to pay.'

From the singing of the late John Reilly from Boyle, Co. Roscommon. There are literally hundreds of versions of this song worldwide, some of which are very well known, like "The Whistling Gypsy" and "The Ballad of Gypsy Daly", but this, I think, is one of the outstanding versions. I started singing it around 1969. The song flows beautifully into Rory Dall Ó Catháin's "Tabhair dom do Lámh".

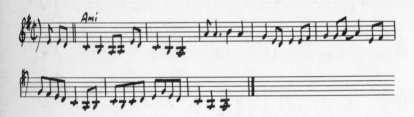

Ah there were three ould gypsies came to our hall door.
They came brave and boldly-o.
And there's one sang high and the other sang low.
And the lady sang the raggle taggle gypsy-o.

It was upstairs downstairs the lady went,
Put on her suit of leather-o,
And it was the cry all around her door,
'She's away with the raggle taggle gypsy-o'.

It was late that night though the lord came in
Enquiring for his lady-o,
And the servant girl's reply to him was,
'She's away with the raggle taggle gypsy-o.'

'Oh then saddle for me, me milk white steed,
Me big horse is not speedy-o,
And I will ride and I'll seek me bride.
She's away with the raggle taggle gypsy-o.'

Oh then he rode east and he rode west
He rode north and south also,
But when he rode to the wide open field
It was there that he spied his lady-o.

'Ara, why do you leave your house and your lands?
Why do you leave your money-o?
Why do you leave your only wedded lord
All for the raggle taggle gypsy-o?'

'Yerra, what do I care for me house and me land?
What do I care for money-o?
Yerra what do I care for me only wedded lord?
I'm away with the raggle taggle gypsy-o.'

'It was there last night you'd a goose feather bed,
Blankets drawn so comely-o,
But tonight you lie in a wide open field
In the arms of the raggle taggle gypsy-o.'

'Yerra what do I care for me goose feather bed?
Yerra what do I care for blankets-o?
What do I care for me only wedded lord?
I'm away with the raggle taggle gypsy-o.

'Oh for you rode east when I rode west,
You rode high and I rode low.
I'd rather have a kiss of the yellow gypsy's lips
Than all the cash and money-o.'

Dark Eyed Sailor

From the singing of Andy Rynne from Prosperous, Co. Kildare, a man from whom
I learned many songs.

As I went a walking one evening fair,
It being the summer, to take the air,
Oh I spied a female with a sailor boy,
And I stood to listen, and I stood to
    listen,
To hear what they might say.

He said, 'Young maid, why do you roam
So all alone by yonder lea?'
Oh she heaved a sigh and the tears did
    roll:
'For my dark eyed sailor, for my dark
    eyed sailor,
He ploughs the stormy seas.'

He said, 'You can drive him from your
    mind,
For another young man you surely will
    find.
Love turns aside and it soon grows cold
Like a winter's morning, like a winter's
    morning.
The hills are white with snow.'

She said, 'I'll not forsake my dear
Although we are parted for manys the
    year,
For gentle he was, not a rake like you
To induce a maiden, to induce a maiden,
To slight the jacket blue.'

One half of the ring did young William
    show.
She ran distracted in grief and woe
Saying, 'William, William, I have gold in
    store
For my dark eyed sailor, for my dark
    eyed sailor.
He has come home again.'

There is a cottage by yonder lea.
The couple live there and do agree.
So maids be true when your love's at sea.
For a stormy morning, for a stormy
    morning
Brings on a sunny day.

This is one of the first songs I wrote and is based on a fragment of a song I came across in a book in about 1964.

Oh I wish I was in England,
In France or even in Spain
Or wherever dwells my own true love
For to hold her near again —
Wherever dwells my own true love
For to hold her near again.

Oh long time I have been roaming
In country and in town
But never in my wandering met
A maid with such renown —
Never in my wandering met
A maid with such renown.

Until I met my true love
On the slopes of Knocknashee,
Her brown hair in the howling wind
A-blowing wild and free —
Her brown hair in the howling wind
A-blowing wild and free.

Oh my true love she did promise me
Some land with rambling kine
And on her ample pasture land
To build a mansion fine —
And on her ample pasture land
To build a mansion fine.

Oh and then my love she left me
And she wandered far away
And I've been searching for my love
For many's the night and day —
I've been searching for my love
For many's the night and day.

Oh I wish that I was in England
Or wherever she may be
That I could go and call her name
And together we would be —
That I could go and call her name
And together we would be.

I heard a version of this song sung by Davy Graham. There are also versions sung by a lot of the old American blues people; I came across this version in a book and started singing it about 1966.

As I was a walking down by the
  Lock Hospital —
Cold was the morning and dark was
  the day —
I spied a young squaddie wrapped up in
  white linen,
Wrapped up in white linen as cold as
  the day.

Chorus

So play the drums slowly, play the pipes
  lowly,
Sound the death march as you carry him
  along,
And over his coffin throw a bunch of
  white laurels
For he's a young soldier cut down in his
  prime.

Oh father, dear mother, come sit you
  down by me,
Sit you down by me and pity my sad
  plight,
For me body is injured and sadly
  disordered,

All by a young girl me own heart's
  delight.

Chorus

Get six of me comrades to carry me
  coffin,
Get six of me comrades to carry me on
  high,
And let every one hold a bunch of white
  roses
So no one will notice as we pass
  them by.

Chorus

All over his headstone these words they
  were written:
'All you young fellows take warning
  from me.
Beware of the flash girls that roam
  through the city
For the girls of the city were the ruin
  of me.'

Chorus

This song, which I learned about 1970, was written by Patrick Galvin, a Cork playwright now living in Belfast. Liam Weldon sings a lovely variation.

Chorus
Where oh where is our James Connolly?
Where oh where is that gallant man?
He's gone to organise the union that working men
They might be free.

Then who, then who will lead the van?
Then who, then who will lead the van?
Who but our James Connolly,
The hero of the working man.

Who will carry high the burning flag?
Who will carry high the burning flag?
Who but our James Connolly
Could carry high the burning flag.

Oh they carried him up to the jail,
They carried him up to the jail,
And they shot him down on a bright May morning
And quickly laid him in his gore.

Who mourns the death of this great man?
Who mourns the death of this great man?
Oh bury me down in yon green garden
With union men on every side.

Oh they buried him down in yon green garden
With union men on every side
And they swore they would form a mighty weapon
That James Connolly's name could be filled with pride.

Chorus

The Hackler from Grouse Hall

From Colm O'Loughlin's collection of Irish street ballads, though I don't sing the full version here. Grouse Hall is in County Cavan. There is another song which is an answer by the sergeant to all the things alleged in the song. I have been singing this one since about 1968; it was a favourite of Bobby Sands' and I note the mention of 'Hackler' in 'McIlhatton'. (see *Ride On* 1984)

I am a roving hackler lad that loves the shamrock shore.
Me name is Pat McDonald and me age is eighty-four.
Beloved and well respected by me neighbours one and all,
On St Patrick's Day, oh, I would like to stray around Lavey and Grouse Hall.

When I was young I danced and sung and drank strong whiskey too
In sheebeen shop that sold a drop o' real oul mountain dew.
With poitín still on every hill the peelers have no call.
Round sweet Stradone I am well known, round Lavey and Grouse Hall.

I used to go from town to town for hacklin' was my trade,
Nor can deny I thought that I an honest living made.
Where'er I strayed by night or day the youth would always call
To have the crack with Paddy Jack, the hackler from Grouse Hall.

I think it strange how very much the times have changed of late.
Coercion now is all the row with peelers on their bate.
To take a glass is now alas the greatest crime of all,
Oh since Balfour placed that hungry beast, the sergeant from Grouse Hall.

That busy tool of Castle rule, he wanders night and day.
He'll take a goat all by the throat for want of better prey.
The nasty skunk, he'll say you're drunk though you've had none at all.
There is no peace around the place since he came to Grouse Hall.

It was on pretence of this offence he dragged me off to jail,
Alone to dwell in a cold cell me fortune to bewail,
Me hoary head on a plank bed; such wrongs for vengeance call.
He'll rue the day he dragged away the hackler from Grouse Hall.

He'll run pell-mell down into hell to search for poitín there
And won't be loath to swear an oath he found it in Killikere.
He'll search your bed from foot to head, sheet, blankets, tick and all.
Your wife undressed must leave the nest for Jenny from Grouse Hall.

Come old and young, clear up your lung and sing this little song.
Come join with me and let them see you all resent the wrong,
And while I live I'll always give a prayer for his downfall,
And when I die I don't deny I'll haunt him from Grouse Hall.

I learned this song from Tony Small while in a squat in Finsbury Park, London about 1968.

It was early spring time, when the strike
  was on,
You drove us miners out of our doors,
Out of the houses that the company
  owned
Into the tents of the little Ludlow.

We were worried bad about our children.
State troopers guarded the railway bridge.
Every once in a while a bullet would fly,
Kick up gravel around our feet.

We were so afraid that you'd kill
  our children
That we dug a cave that was seven
  foot deep,
Took the children and the pregnant
  women
Down inside the cave to sleep.

It was late that night; the soldiers waited
Till all us miners were asleep,
Crept around our little camptown
And soaked our tents in kerosene.

Well they struck a match and the blaze
  had started.
They pulled the triggers on their
  gatling guns.
Made a run for the children but the
  fireball stopped me
And thirteen children died from
  their guns.

I took my blanket to the wire fence corner
And I watched the flames till the blaze
  died down.
Saw some folks drag their belongings
While your bullets killed them all around.

Well I rang the governor for to phone up
  the president,
Tell him call off the National Guard,
But the National Guard belonged to the
  governor
So I guess he didn't try very hard.

I never will forget the looks on the faces
Of the men and women that awful day
As they stood around to preach the
  funeral
And lay the corpses of the dead away.

Well the women from Trinidad took some
  potatoes
Up to Wallensburg in a little cart.
They sold the potatoes and they brought
  some guns back
And put a gun in every hand.

'Twas late that night the troopers charged
  us —
They didn't know that we had guns —
And the red-necked miners, they shot the
  soldiers.
You should have seen them poor boys
  run.

We took some cement and walled the
  cave up
Where the thirteen little children died.
I thanked God for the Mine Workers
  Union
And then I hung my head and cried.

I believe this was written by a man from Sixmilebridge in County Clare and I think the author may have been Bobby Gleeson; I learned it when I was working as a bank official in Tulla in Co. Clare.

Last night as I lay dreaming of pleasant days gone by,
Me mind being bent on rambling, to Ireland I did fly.
I stepped on board a vision and I followed with a will
And I shortly came to anchor at the cross of Spancil Hill.

Delighted by the novelty, enchanted by the scene
Where in my early boyhood often I had been,
I thought I heard a murmur and I think I hear it still.
It's the little stream of water that flows down Spancil Hill.

To amuse a passing fancy I lay down on the ground
Where all my school companions they shortly gathered round.
When we were home returning we danced with bright goodwill
To Martin Moylan's music at the cross of Spancil Hill.

It being on the 23rd of June, the day before the fair,
When Ireland's sons and daughters and friends assembled there,
The young, the old, the brave and the bold, they came to sport and kill.
There were curious combinations at the fair of Spancil Hill.

I went to see my neighbours to hear what they might say.
The old ones were all dead and gone, the young ones worn and grey.
I met with the tailor Quigley, he's as bold as ever still;
Sure he used to make my britches when I lived in Spancil Hill.

I paid a flying visit to my first and only love.
She's white as any lily and gentle as a dove.
She threw her arms around me saying, 'Johnny, I love you still.'
Oh she's Mac the ranger's daughter and the pride of Spancil Hill.

Oh I dreamt I stooped and kissed her as in the days of yore.
She said, 'Johnny, you're only joking as many's the time before.'
The cock crew in the morning, he crew both loud and shrill.
And I woke in California many miles from Spancil Hill.

From the singing of Andy Rynne of Prosperous; I always enjoy singing this despite thousands of performances. The Cliffs of Dooneen are situated at the back of Ballybunion.

You may travel far, far from your own native home,
Far away o'er the mountains, far away o'er the foam,
But of all the fine places that I've ever been
Oh there's none to compare with the Cliffs of Dooneen.

It's a nice place to be on a fine summer's day,
Watching all the wild flowers that ne'er do decay.
Oh the hare and lofty pheasant are plain to be seen,
Making homes for their young round the Cliffs of Dooneen.

Take a view o'er the mountains, fine sights you'll see there.
You'll see the high rocky mountains on the west coast of Clare.
Oh the towns of Kilkee and Kilrush can be seen
From the high rocky slopes of the Cliffs of Dooneen.

Fare thee well to Dooneen, fare thee well for a while,
And to all the fine people I'm leaving behind,
To the streams and the meadows where late I have been
And the high rocky slopes of the Cliffs of Dooneen.

Currach, Aran Islands. Fergus Bourke

I learned this song from Mike Harding, Manchester, with whom I lived for six months in 1968.

When first from boyhood I came to
    a man
To ramble the nation through I soon
    began.
Oh the ramblin' thought that came into
    me mind,
So they christened me Ramblin'
    Robin Oh,
So they christened me Ramblin'
    Robin Oh.

O'er hills and o'er mountains I used to go.
I slept in the woods where there's frost
    and there's snow.
No anxiety ever came into me mind.
So contented was Ramblin' Robin Oh,
So contented was Ramblin' Robin Oh.

The wind and the rain oh they blew me
    quite cold.
Me parents at home they were both
    growing old.
Oh me father did weep and me mother
    did cry
For the loss of their Ramblin' Robin Oh,
For the loss of their Ramblin' Robin Oh.

When sixteen long years they were over
    and past
Me poor mother's sorrow was ended
    at last
And me father the nation did range
    through and through
Oh in search of his Ramblin' Robin Oh,
Oh in search of his Ramblin' Robin Oh.

When all me past follies they came to
    an end
To me own little village I did attend.
Oh the neighbours they told me me
    parents were dead
Filled with grief for their Ramblin'
    Robin Oh,
Filled with grief for their Ramblin'
    Robin Oh.

Oh where shall I wander and where shall
    I go?
Me heart it is filled with sorrow and woe.
Oh the nation I'll wander through and
    through
And an end put to Ramblin' Robin Oh.
And an end put to Ramblin' Robin Oh.

From the singing of Ewan McColl who also wrote the song; I learned it about 1971.

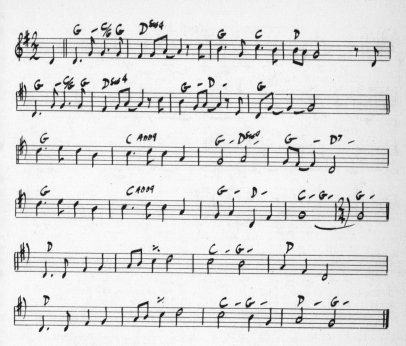

I met my love near Woolwich Pier
Beneath the big pier standing
All the love I felt for her
It passed all understanding.

Took her sailing on the river,
Flow sweet river flow.
London town was mine to give her,
Sweet Thames flows softly.

Made the Thames into a crown,
Flow sweet river flow.
Made a brooch of silver town,
Sweet Thames flows softly.

From Shadwell dock to Nine-Elms reach,
We cheek to cheek were dancing.
Her necklace made of London bridge,
Her beauty was enhancing.

Kissed her once again at Wopping,
Flow sweet river flow,
After that there was no stopping,
Sweet Thames flows softly.

Gave at Richmond Park a twist,
Flow sweet river flow,
Into a bracelet for her wrist,
Sweet Thames flows softly.

But now alas the tide has changed;
My love she has gone from me.
Winter's frost has touched my heart
And put a blight upon me.

Creeping fog is on the river,
Flow sweet river flow.
Sun and moon and stars gone with her,
Sweet Thames flows softly.

Swift the Thames flows to the sea,
Flow sweet river flow,
Bearing ships and part of me,
Sweet Thames flows softly.

Follow Me up to Carlow

An old ballad which I have been singing since about 1960; we don't write them like this any more.

Lift Mac Cahir Óg your face,
Brooding o'er the old disgrace
That black Fitzwilliam stormed your place,
Drove you to the fern.

Grey said victory was sure,
Soon the firebrand he'd secure,
Until he met at Glenmalure
With Fiach MacHugh O'Byrne.

Chorus
Curse and swear, Lord Kildare.
Fiach will do what Fiach will dare.
Now, Fitzwilliam, have a care,
Fallen is your star low.
Up with halberd, out with sword,
On we'll go for, by the Lord,
Fiach MacHugh has given the word;
Follow me up to Carlow.

See the swords at Glen Imaal
They flash all over the English pale
See all the children of the Gael
Beneath O'Byrne's banners.

Rooster of a fighting stock
Would you let a Saxon cock
Crow out upon an Irish rock?
Fly up and teach him manners.

Chorus

From Tassagart to Clonmore
There flows a stream of Saxon gore.
Well great is Rory Óg O More
At sending the loons to Hades.

White is sick, Grey is fled;
Now for black Fitzwilliam's head.
We'll send it over dripping red
To Queen Liza and her ladies.

Chorus

From the singing of John Reilly of Boyle, Co. Roscommon. This is a travelling song based on a biblical story. The older travellers are very reluctant to sing it and I have known it to evoke strange sensations.

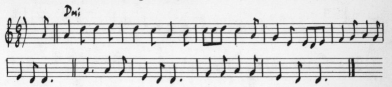

A gentleman was passing by.
He asked for a drink as he got dry
At the well below the valley-o.

Chorus
Green grows the lily-o
Right among the bushes-o

'Me cup is full up to the brim.
If I were to stoop
I might fall in.'

Chorus

'If your true love was passing by
You'd fill him a drink as he got dry
At the well below the valley-o.'

Chorus

She swore by grass, she swore by corn,
That her true love had never been born
At the well below the valley-o.

Chorus

He said, 'Young maid, your swearing
    wrong,
For six fine children you had born
At the well below the valley-o.'

Chorus

'If you be a man of noble fame,
You'll tell to me the father of them.
At the well below the valley-o.'

Chorus

'There's two of them by your Uncle Dan
At the well below the valley-o.'

Chorus

'Another two by your brother John
At the well below the valley-o.'

Chorus

'Another two by your father dear
At the well below the valley-o.'

Chorus

'If you be a man of noble esteem,
You'll tell to me what did happen to them
At the well below the valley-o.'

Chorus

'There's two buried 'neath the stable door
At the well below the valley-o.'

Chorus

'Another two near the kitchen door
At the well below the valley-o.'

Chorus

'Another two buried beneath the well
At the well below the valley-o.'

Chorus

'If you be a son of noble fame,
You tell to me what'll happen meself
At the well below the valley-o.'

Chorus

'You'll be seven years a-ringing the bell
At the well below the valley-o.'

Chorus

'You'll be seven more a-burning in hell
At the well below the valley-o.'

Chorus

'I'll be seven years a ringing the bell
But the lord above me save me soul
From burning in hell
At the well below the valley-o.'

Chorus

From the singing of Andy Rynne of Prosperous, Co. Kildare, who turned in his whistle in favour of a stethoscope.

'And who are you me pretty fair maid and who are you me honey?
Who are you me pretty fair maid and who are you me honey?'
She answered me quite modestly, 'I am me mother's darling.'

Chorus
With me toor ay ah faddle diddle da, diri fal de diddle derrio.

'And will you come to me mother's house, when the moon is shining clearly?
Oh and will you come to me mother's house, when the moon is shining clearly?
I'll open the door and I'll let you in and divil the one will hear us.'

Chorus

So I went to her house in the middle of the night when the moon was shining clearly.
Oh I went to her house in the middle of the night when the moon was shining clearly.
She opened the door and let me in and divil the one did hear us.

Chorus

She took me horse by the bridle and the bit and she led him to the stable.
Oh she took me horse by the bridle and the bit and she led him to the stable.
'And there's plenty of oats for the soldier's horse to eat them if he's able.'

Chorus

And she took me by the lily white hand and she led me to the table.
She took me by the lily white hand and she led me to the table,
Saying, 'There's plenty of wine for the soldier boy, so drink it if you're able.'

Chorus

Then I got up and I made the bed and I made it nice and easy.
Oh then I got up and I made the bed and I made it nice and easy.
I got up and I laid her down saying, 'Lassie, are ye able?'

Chorus

And there we lay till the break of the day and divil the one did hear us.
Oh and there we lay till the break of the day and divil the one did hear us.
Then I arose and put on me clothes saying, 'Lassie, I must leave you.'

Chorus

'And when will you return again and when will we get married?
And when will you return again and when will we get married?'
'When broken shells make Christmas bells, we might well get married.'

Chorus

From Andy Irvine. A song from the borders of Limerick and Tipperary, which should always be sung around Limerick Junction.

One fine summer's morning both gallant and gay
Twenty-four ladies were out on the quay
And a regiment of soldiers, it did pass them by;
A drummer, and one of them soon caught his eye.

He went to his comrade and to him did say,
'Twenty-four ladies I saw yesterday.
Oh and one of them ladies she has me heart won
And if she denies me I'm surely undone.'

'Go to this lady and tell her your mind,
Tell her she's wounded your poor heart inside.
Go and tell her she's wounded your poor heart full sore,
And if she denies you what can she do more.'

So early next morning this young man arose,
Dressed himself up in a fine suit of clothes.
With a watch in his pocket and a cane in his hand,
Saluting the ladies, he walked down the strand.

He went up to her and he said, 'Pardon me.
Pardon me, lady, for making so free.
Oh, me fine honoured lady, you have my heart won
And if you deny me I'm surely undone.'

'Be off, little drummer, now what do you mean?
I'm the lord's daughter of Ballykisteen.
Oh I'm the lord's daughter that's honoured, do you see?
Go off, little drummer, you're making too free.'

He put on his hat and he bade her farewell
Saying, 'I'll send me soul down to heaven or hell,
For with this long pistol that hangs by my side.
Oh I'll put an end to me own dreary life.'

'Come back, little drummer, and don't take it ill
For I do not want to be guilty of sin,
To be guilty of innocent blood for to spill.
Come back, little drummer, I'm here at your will.

'And we'll hire a car and to Bansha we'll go.
There we'll be married in spite of our foes.
Oh for what can they say when it's over and done
But I fell in love with the roll of your drum.'

I learned this song in 1966 from the singing of Mike Waterson of Hull.
Ponchartrain is situated outside New Orleans and this is reputed to be an American
Civil War song about a soldier who found himself on the wrong side of the line
after the truce and was helped out of his predicament by a woman.

It was one fine March morning I bid New Orleans adieu
And I took the road to Jackson town, my fortune to renew.
I cursed all foreign money, no credit could I gain,
Which filled me heart with longing for
The lakes of Ponchartrain.

I stepped on board of a railroad car beneath the morning sun.
I rode the rods till evening and I laid me down again.
All strangers there no friends to me till a dark girl towards me came
And I fell in love with the Creole girl
By the lakes of Ponchartrain.

I said, 'Me pretty Creole girl, me money here's no good.
If it weren't for the alligators, I'd sleep out in the wood.'
'You're welcome here, kind stranger, from such sad thoughts refrain,
For me Mammy welcomes strangers
By the lakes of Ponchartrain.'

She took me into her Mammy's house, and treated me right well.
The hair upon her shoulders in jet black ringlets fell.
To try and paint her beauty, I'm sure 'twould be in vain,
So handsome was my Creole girl
By the lakes of Ponchartrain.

I asked her if she'd marry me. She said that ne'er could be
For she had got a lover and he was far at sea.
She said that she would wait for him and true she would remain
Till he'd return to his Creole girl
On the lakes of Ponchartrain.

It's fare thee well, me Creole girl, I never may see you more.
I'll ne'er forget your kindness in the cottage by the shore
And at each social gathering, a flowing bowl I'll drain
And I'll drink a health to my Creole girl
By the lakes of Ponchartrain.

Ewan McColl wrote this about Tim Evans, who was not the last innocent man to be executed.

Tim Evans was a prisoner down in his prison cell.
Those who read about his crime condemned his soul to hell.
Go down, you murderer, go down.
For the killing of his own dear wife and the murder of his child
The jury found him guilty and the hanging judge he smiled,
Go down, you murderer, go down.

They took Tim Evans from the dock and they led him to a cell,
They closed the door behind his back saying, 'Damn your soul to hell.'
Go down, you murderer, go down.
Tim Evans walked around the yard and the screws they walked behind.
He saw the sky above the wall but knew no peace of mind.
Go down, you murderer, go down.

The governor came to his cell with the chaplain by his side
Saying, 'Your appeal has been turned down, prepare yourself to die.'
Go down, you murderer, go down.
They took Tim Evans to the place where the hangman did prepare.
They tied the rope around his neck, put the knot behind his ear.
Go down, you murderer, go down.

A thousand lags were screaming and banging at their doors.
Tim Evans didn't hear them, he was dead forever more.
Go down, you murderer, go down.
They sent Tim Evans to the drop for a crime he didn't do;
It's Christie was the murderer, the judge and jury too.
Go down, you murderers, go down.
Go down, you murderers, go down.
Go down, you murderers, go down.

John Reilly, whose singing still inspires me many years after his death; he had a style of putting it over that was lovely to listen to.

Singing, 'What put the blood on your
    right shoulder?
And, son, come tell it to me, to me.
Son, come tell it to me to me.'
'Oh, that is the blood of a hare, Mama,
And you may pardon me —
You may pardon me.'

Saying, 'The blood of a hare never ran so
    red.'
Saying, 'Son, come tell it on to me, to me.
Son, come tell it on to me.'
'Oh, that is the blood of me youngest
    brother
And you may pardon me —
You may pardon me.'

Singing, 'What came between you and
    your youngest brother?
Oh, son, come tell it on to me, to me.
Son, come tell it on to me.'
'It was all from the cutting of a hazel
    rod
That never will grow a tree —
Never will grow a tree.'

Singing, 'What will you do with your
    darling wife?
Oh, son, come tell it on to me, to me.
Son, come tell it on to me.'
'She will leave her foot down on a ship's
    board
And she'll sail it after me —
Sail right after me.'

Singing, 'What will you do with your two
    fine children?
Oh, son, come tell it on to me, to me.
Son, come tell it on to me.'
'I'll give one to me mammy and the
    other to me daddy.
It'll keep them company —
Keep them company.'

Singing, 'What will you do with your
    loving house?
And, son, come tell it on to me, to me.
Son, come tell it on to me.'
'I will leave it there to the birds of the air
For to mourn and sing for me —
To mourn and sing for me.'

Singing, 'What will you do with your
    two greyhounds?
And, son, come tell it on to me, to me.
Son, come tell it on to me.'
'I will take the lead from around their
    necks
And no more they'll hunt for me —
No more they'll hunt for me.'

Singing, 'What will you do with your two
    racehorses?
And, son, come tell it on to me, to me.
Son, come tell it on to me.'
'I will take the bridle from their necks
And no more they'll race for me,
    for me —
No more they'll race for me.'

From the collection of Tom Munnelly, who collected it in Kerry.

In Scartaglen there lived a lass
And every Sunday after mass
She would go and take a glass
Before going home by Bearna.

We won't go home along the road
For fear that you might act the rogue.
Won't go home along the road;
We'll go home by Bearna.

We won't go home across the fields.
The big thornins could stick in your
     heels.
We won't go home across the fields;
We'll go home by Bearna.

We won't go home around the glen
For fear your blood might rise again.
Won't go home around the glen,
But we'll go home by Bearna.

We won't go down the milk boreen.
The night is bright we might be seen.
We won't go down the milk boreen,
But we'll go home by Bearna.

We won't go home across the bog
In fear we might meet Kearney's dog.
We won't go home across the bog,
But we'll go home by Bearna.

'Go! Move! Shift!' Eamonn O'Dwyer (Report)

Or **'Go, Move, Shift'**; written by Ewan McColl for a series he wrote on the hardships of the travelling people. When I sing this song I always remember a picket I saw in Galway where local people were demanding the travellers move and simultaneously saying the rosary.

Born in the middle of the afternoon
In a horsedrawn carriage on the old A5.
The big twelve wheeler shook my bed,
'You can't stay here,' the policeman said.

Chorus
'You'd better get born in some place else.
Move along, get along,
Move along, get along,
Go! Move! Shift!'

Born on the common by a building site
Where the ground was rutted by the trail
    of wheels
The local Christian said to me,
'You'll lower the price of property.'

Chorus

Born at potato picking time
In a tent in a tatie field.
The farmer said, 'The work's all done,
It's time that you was moving on.'

Chorus

Born at the back of a hawthorn hedge
Where the frost lay on the ground.
No eastern kings came bearing gifts.
Instead the order came to shift.

Chorus

The eastern sky was full of stars
And one shone brighter than the rest.
The wise men came so stern and strict
And brought the orders to evict.

Chorus

Wagon, tent or trailer born,
Last month, last year or in far off days.
Born here or a thousand miles away
There's always men nearby who'll say,

Chorus

From the singing of Mike Waterson from Hull in Yorkshire.

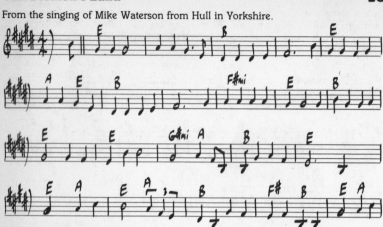

Me and three more went out one night
Into Squire Noble's park.
We were hoping we might get some
  game,
The night been proven dark.
It being our bad misfortune
They trepanned us with speed
And sent us down to Warwick jail,
Did cause our hearts to bleed.

Chorus
Young men all be aware,
  lest you be drawn into a snare.
Young men all be aware,
  lest you be drawn into a snare.

About the 5th of March, me boys,
At the bar we did appear.
Like Job we stood with patience
Our sentence to hear there.
There being no witness standing
Our case it did go hard.
Our sentence was for fourteen years
Straight away being sent on board.

Chorus

The ship that bore us from the land
The Speedwell was her name.
For full five months and upwards
We ploughed the raging main.
We saw no land or harbour,
I tell you it's no lie.
All around us one black ocean,
Above us one blue sky.

Chorus

About the 5th of August
It's then we made the land.
At five next morning,
They tied us hand to hand.
To see our fellow sufferance
Filled me heart with woe.
There's some chained to the harrow,
And others to the plough.

Chorus

To see our fellow sufferance
Filled me heart with woe.
For they'd leather smocks and lindsay
  shorts,
Their feet and hands were bare.
They tied them up two by two
Like horses in a dray.
The driver he stood over them
With his malacca cane.

Chorus

Come all you wild and reckless youths
That listen unto me,
Mark you well the story that I tell,
Guard your destiny.
It's all about transported lads,
As you will understand,
The hardships we did undergo,
Going to Van Diemen's Land.

Chorus

I learned this from Muriel Graves from the Lake District in England in a folk club in 1967. Little did I think that by bringing it back to Ireland I was going to write a page in the annals of folk history and launch Foster and Allen to stardom.

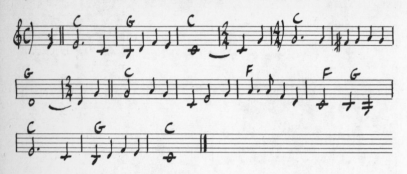

Come all you maidens young and fair,
All you that are blooming in your prime.
Oh always beware
And keep your garden fair.
Let no man steal away your thyme.

Chorus
For thyme it is a precious thing
And thyme brings all things to my mind.
Oh thyme with all its labours
Along with all its joys,
Thyme brings all things to my mind.

Oh once I had a bunch of thyme,
I thought it never would decay,
But on came a lusty sailor
Who chanced to pass that way.
He stole my bunch of thyme away.

The sailor gave to me a rose
A rose that never will decay.
He gave it to me
To keep me well minded
Of when he stole my thyme away.

So come all you maidens young and fair,
Oh you that are blooming in your prime,
Oh always beware
And keep your garden fair.
Let no man steal away your thyme.

Chorus

I heard this while living in Halifax in Yorkshire in about 1969. Hull and Halifax were two of the many towns in Yorkshire where you could be hanged for begging. It is a song of the industrial revolution but is based on a much older Yorkshire poem.

It's hard when folks can't get their work
Where they've been bred and born.
When I was young I used to think
I'd bide 'mid the roots and the corn,
But I've been forced to flee to town.
Here's my litany.
From Hull and Halifax and Hell,
Good Lord deliver me.

When I was courting Mary Anne
The old squire he said one day,
'I've got no room for wedded folks.
Choose, Will, to wed or stay.'
I could not leave the girl I loved
So to town I had to flee.
From Hull and Halifax and Hell,
Good Lord deliver me.

I've worked in Leeds and Huddersfield
Where I've addled honest brass.
In Bradford, Keighley, Rotherham,
I've left me bairns and lass.
I've travelled all three ridings round
And once I've been to sea.
From Hull and Halifax and Hell,
Good Lord deliver me.

I've been through Sheffield lanes at night.
'Twas just like being to Hell.
The furnaces thrust out tongues of flame
That roared like the wind o'er the field.
I've sammed up coal in Barnsley Pit
With mud up to me knee.
From Hull and Halifax and Hell,
Good Lord deliver me.

I've seen grey fog creep o'er Leeds brig
As thick as Bastille soup.
I've been where folks are stowed away
Like chickens in a coop.
I've seen snow fall on Bradford beck
As black as 'ere ebony.
From Hull and Halifax and Hell,
Good Lord deliver me.

Now my children all have flown
To the country I'll go back.
There'll be forty miles of heathery moor
'Twixt me and the coal pit slack.
Oft at night as we sit 'round the fire
We think of the misery.
From Hull and Halifax and Hell,
Good Lord deliver me.

Three verses of this were written by Patsy Halloran from Clonmel, Co. Tipperary, and I learned them in 1963; I added the last verse myself.

'I joined the Flying Column in 1916,
In Cork with Sean Moylan, in Tipperary with Dan Breen.
Arrested by Free Staters and sentenced to die.
Farewell to Tipperary,' said the Galtee mountain boy.

'We went across the valleys and over the hilltops green,
Where we met with Dinny Lacey, Sean Hogan and Dan Breen,
Sean Moylan and his gallant men that kept the flag flying high.
Farewell to Tipperary,' said the Galtee mountain boy.

'We tracked the Dublin mountains, we were rebels on the run.
Though hunted night and morning, we were outlaws but free men.
We tracked the Wicklow mountains as the sun was shining high,
Farewell to Tipperary,' said the Galtee mountain boy.

'I bid farewell to old Clonmel that I never more will see
And through the Galtee mountains that oft times sheltered me,
The men who fought for their liberty and who died without a sigh.
May their cause be ne'er forgotten,' said the Galtee mountain boy.

A version in which I used old lyrics, added some lyrics of my own and put them together with a tune from the singing of Nick Jones.

It fell upon a holy day,
As many is in the year,
Musgrave to the church did go
To see fine ladies there.

And some were dressed in velvet red
And some in velvet pale
And then came Lord Barnard's wife,
The fairest among them all.

She cast an eye on the Little Musgrave
As bright as the summer sun.
Said Musgrave unto himself,
'This lady's heart I've won.'

'I have loved you, fair lady,
For long and many's the day.'
'And I have loved you, little Musgrave,
And never a word did say.

'I have a bower in Bucklesfordberry.
It's my heart's delight.
I'll take you back there with me
If you'll lie in my arms tonight.'

But standing by was a little foot page.
From the ladies coach he ran:
'Though I am a lady's page,
I am Lord Barnard's man.'

'Me Lord Barnard will hear of this
Oh whether I sink or swim.'
Everywhere the bridge was broke
He'd enter the water and swim.

'Oh, me Lord Barnard, me Lord Barnard,
You are a man of life.
Little Musgrave, he's at Bucklesfordberry
Asleep with your wedded wife.'

'If this is true, me little foot page,
This thing that you tell me,
All the gold in Bucklesfordberry
I gladly will give to thee.

'But if this be a lie, me little foot page,
This thing that you tell me,
From the highest tree in Bucklesfordberry,
Hanged you will be.

'Go saddle me the black,' he said.
'Go saddle me the grey,
And sound not your horns,' he said,
'Lest our coming you betray.'

But there was a man in Lord Barnard's
        train
Who loved the Little Musgrave.
He blew his born both loud and shrill,
'Away, Musgrave, Away!'

'I think I hear the morning cock,
I think I hear the jay,
I think I hear Lord Barnard's men.
I wish I was away.'

'Be still, be still, my Little Musgrave,
Hug me from the cold.
It's nothing but the shepherd lad
A-bringing his flock to fold.'

'Is not your hawk upon its perch
Your steed eats oats and hay
And you a lady in your arms
And yet you'd go away?'

He's turned her around and he's kissed
  her twice
And then they fell asleep.
When they awoke, Lord Barnard's men
Were standing at their feet.

'How do you like me bed' he said,
'And how do you like me sheets?
How do you like me fair lady
That lies in your arms asleep?'

'It's well I like your bed,' he said,
'And great it gives me pain.
I'd gladly give one hundred pounds
To be on yonder plain.'

'Rise up, rise up, Little Musgrave,
Rise up and then put on.
It'll not be said in this country
I slayed a naked man.'

So slowly, slowly he got up,
So slowly he put on,
Slowly down the stairs,
Thinking to be slain.

'There are two swords down by my side
And dear they cost me purse.
You can have the best of them
And I will take the worst.'

Well the first stroke that Little Musgrave
  struck
It hurt Lord Barnard sore,
But the next stroke Lord Barnard struck,
Little Musgrave ne'er struck more.

And then up spoke the lady fair
From the bed whereon she lay,
'Although you're dead, me Little
  Musgrave,
Still for you I'll pray.'

'How do you like his cheeks?' he said.
'How do you like his chin?
How do you like his dead body,
Now there's no life within?'

'It's more I like his cheeks,' she cried,
'And more I want his chin.
It's more I love that dead body
Than all your kith and kin.'

He's taken out his long long sword
To strike the mortal blow.
Through and through the lady's heart
The cold steel it did go.

'A grave, a grave,' Lord Barnard cried,
'To put these lovers in.
Put me lady on the upper hand
She came from better kin.'

'For I've just killed the finest knight
That ever rode a steed
And I've just killed the finest lady
That ever did a woman's deed.'

It fell upon a holy day,
As many in the year,
Musgrave to the church did go
To see fine ladies there.

Wave Up To The Shore

Written by Barry Moore.

A daffodil is born and rises in the spring.
It opens out its beauty to hear the cricket sing,
But as quick as it does grow it decays away so soon
And before the summer sunshine has reached its golden noon,
Before the summer sunshine has reached its golden noon.

A stream it does rise in the mountain so tall.
It swells into a river as gently it does fall.
It meanders through valley, through city and through town
And in the boundless ocean, this river it is drowned,
And in the boundless ocean, this river it is drowned.

On the sea the winds do rage and the waves grow so high,
White around their surface as they reach up to the sky,
But soon the waves grow gentle, no longer do they roar
As they make their lonesome passageway up to the pebble shore,
As they make their lonesome passageway up to the pebble shore.

If I was like a daffodil, so fair upon the ground,
Or like a winding river with its sweet and mellow sound,
Like a wave up to the shore, like a river into the sea,
I'd lay down in my resting place, contented there I would be,
I'd lay down in my resting place, and contented I would be.

I first heard this song in 1968 in Jersey in the Channel Islands where it was sung by the author Barney Rush, originally from Sallynoggin but now living in Germany. Barney recorded it for me and I had the tape in a drawer for about ten years before I started to sing it. I suppose it has become the best known song in my repertoire.

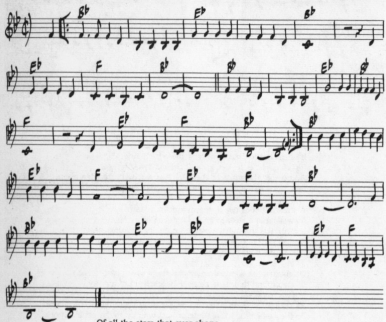

Of all the stars that ever shone
Not one does twinkle like your pale blue eyes,
Like golden corn at harvest time, your hair.
Sailing in my boat the wind gently blows and fills my sail.
Your sweet scented breath is everywhere.

Daylight peeping through the curtains of
The passing night time is your smile.
The sun in the sky is like your laugh.
Come back to me Nancy linger for just a little while.
Since you left these shores I know no peace nor joy.

Chorus
No matter where I wander I'm still haunted by your name.
The portrait of your beauty stays the same.
Standing by the ocean, wondering where you've gone,
If you'll return again.
Where is the ring I gave to Nancy Spain?

On the day in spring when the snow starts to melt and streams to flow
With the birds I'll sing to you a song.
In the while I'll wander down by bluebell grove
Where wild flowers grow
And I'll hope that lovely Nancy will return.

Chorus

Andy, Christy, Juno and Nancy Moore. Colm Henry

I think I saw this first in Colm O'Loughlin's *Irish Street Ballads*; I added bits and pieces of my own and started singing it in about 1974. I taught Dermot from The Bards the song one night on the mailboat and he made a great hit out of it — no better man.

In the town of Athy, one Jeremy Lanigan
Battered away till he hadn't a shilling.
His father died, made him a man again,
Left him a farm and ten acres of ground.

Myself, to be sure, got invitations
For the boys and girls I might ask.
Having been asked, friends and relations
Danced like bees around a sweet cask.

There was lashings of drink, wine for the
ladies,
Potatoes and cake, bacon and tea.
Nolans and Dolans and all the O'Gradys,
Courting the girls and dancing away.

While songs went round as plenty as
water,
The harps that are sounded through
Tara's old hall,
Biddie Grey and the rat catcher's daughter
Singing away at Lanigan's ball.

Chorus

Six long months I spent in Dublin,
Six long months doing nothing at all,
Six long months I spent in Dublin,
Learning to dance for Lanigan's ball.
She stepped out, I stepped in again.
I stepped out and she stepped in again.
She stepped out, I stepped in again,
Learning to dance for Lanigan's ball.

They were doing all kinds of nonsensical
dances
All around in a whirligigig.
Julie and I soon banished their nonsense,
Out on the floor for a reel and a jig.

How the girls all got mad at me
For they thought the ceilings would fall.
I spent six months in Brook's Academy
Learning to dance for Lanigan's ball.

Well the boys were merry and the girls
all hearty
Dancing around in their couples and
groups.
An accident happened; Terence McCarthy,
He put his boot through Miss Finnerty's
hoops.

She fell down in a faint and cried,
'Holy murder!'
Called her brothers and gathered them all.
Carmody swore he'd go no further
Till he got revenge at Lanigan's ball.

Chorus

Boys oh boys 'tis then there was ructions.
I got a belt from Phelim Mc Hugh.
I replied to his introduction,
Kicked up a terrible hullabaloo.

Moloney the piper was near gettin'
smothered;
They leapt on his pipes, bellows, chanter
and all.
Boys and girls all got entangled
And that put an end to Lanigan's ball.

Chorus

Johnny Jump Up

Came to me from Jimmy Crowley from Cork, who I first heard singing it upstairs in a tent.

I'll tell you a story that happened to me
One day as I went down to Youghal by the sea.
The sun it was bright and the day it was warm.
Says I, 'A quiet pint wouldn't do me no harm.'

I went in and I called for a bottle of stout.
Says the barman, 'I'm sorry, all the beer is sold out.
Try whiskey or Paddy, ten years in the wood.'
Says I, 'I'll try cider, I hear that it's good.'

Chorus
Oh never, oh never, oh never again,
If I live to a hundred or a hundred and ten
For I fell to the ground and I couldn't get up
After drinking a quart of the Johnny Jump Up.

After leaving the third I went to the yard
Where I bumped into Brophy, the big civic guard.
'Come here to me, boy, don't you know I'm the law?'
I upped with me fist and I shattered his jaw.

He fell to the ground with his knees doubled up
But it wasn't I hit him, 'twas Johnny Jump Up.
The next thing I met down in Youghal by the sea
Was a cripple on crutches and says he to me,

'I'm afraid of me life I'll be hit by a car.
Won't you help me across to the Railways Men's bar?'
After drinking a quart of that cider so sweet
He threw down his crutches and danced in the street.

I went up the Lee road a friend for to see,
And they call it the mad house in Cork by the Lee,
But I when I got up there, the truth I do tell,
They had the poor bugger locked up in a cell.

Said the guard, testing him, say these words if you can:
'Around the rugged rock the ragged rascal ran.'
'Tell them I'm not crazy, tell them I'm not mad.
It was only a sup of the bottle I had.'

A man died in the Union by the name of McNabb.
They washed him and laid him outside on a slab,
And after O'Connor his measurements did take,
His wife took him home to a bloody fine wake.

About twelve o'clock and the beer it was high
When the corpse he sat up and says he with a sigh,
'I can't get to heaven, they won't let me up,
Till I bring them a quart of the Johnny Jump Up.'

Chorus

I learned this song in Tulla in Co. Clare in Murphy's pub at the top of the hill about 1964 and remember old Mrs Murphy describing to me the funeral of the four young men in 1922 and the atmosphere that was in East Clare at the time. To this day there are marks on the bridge where they were shot down and a stone in memory of them. When I sing this song these days I think of Eamon Byrne, shot down on the North Wall Dublin on 23 November 1982. I first heard John Minogue singing this song.

The dreadful news through Ireland has spread from shore to shore,
For such a deed no living man has ever heard before.
The deeds of Cromwell in his time I'm sure no worse could do
Than those Black and Tans that murdered those four youths in Killaloe.

Three of the four were on the run and searched for all around
Until with this brave Egan from Williamstown was found.
They asked him were the boys inside, to the rebels he proved true,
And because he would not sell the pass he was shot in Killaloe.

On the fourth day of November, that day of sad renown,
They were sold and traced through Galway to that house in Williamstown.
They never got a fighting chance but were captured while asleep
And the way that they ill-treated them would cause your blood to creep.

They shackled them both hands and feet with twines they could not break
And they brought them down to Killaloe by steamer on the lake.
Without clergy, judge or jury, on the bridge they shot them down
And their blood flowed with the Shannon convenient to the town.

With three days of perseverance their bodies they let go.
At 10.00 p.m. their funeral passed through Ogonolloe.
They were kept in Scarriff chapel for two nights and a day.
Now in that place of rest they lie, kind people for them pray.

If you were at their funeral it was an awful sight
To see the local clergy and they all dressed up in white.
Such a sight of these four martyrs in one grave was never seen,
For they died to save the flag of love, the orange, white and green.

Now that they are dead and gone, I hope in peace they'll rest
Like all young Irish martyrs, forever among the blessed.
The day will come when all will know who sold the lives away
Of young McMahon, Rodgers, brave Egan and Kildea.

I cannot recall the source of the song nor where I heard it first but I have been singing it since 1962.

I'm a young fellow that's easy and bold.
In Castletownconnors I'm very well known.
In Newcastlewest I spent many a night
With Kitty, Judy and Mary.

Me father rebuked me for being such a rake,
For spending me time in such frolicsome
 ways.
I ne'er could forget the good nature of June.
Fágaimíd siúd mar a tá sé.

Me parents had taught me to shake and to
 sow,
To plough, to harrow, to reap and to mow.
Me mind being too airy to leave it so low,
I went out in high speculation.

On parchment and paper they taught me to
 write,
In Euclid and grammar they opened me eyes.
In multiplication in truth I was bright.
Fágaimíd siúd mar a tá sé.

If I happen to go to the town of Rathkeel
The girls around me do flock in the square.
Some give me the bottle and others sweet
 cake.
They treat unknown to their parents.

There's one from Askeaton and one from the
 Pike,
Another from Ardagh, me heart is beguiled.
Though being from the mountains her
 stockings are white.
Fágaimíd siúd mar a tá sé.

To quarrel for riches I ne'er was inclined.
The greatest of misers must leave them
 behind.
I get the cow that will never run dry
And milk her by twisting her horns.

John Damer of Shronel had plenty of gold.
Devonshire's treasure was twenty times more.
He's on his back amid pebbles and stones.
Fágaimíd siúd mar a tá sé.

If I happened to go to market in Croom,
With cock in me hat and my pipes in full
 tune,
I'd be welcomed at once and brought up to a
 room
Where Bacchus is sporting with Venus.

There's Biddy and Jane from the town of
 Bruree,
Mary from Bruff and we're all of a spree.
Such a roaming of frocks as there was about
 me.
Fágaimíd siúd mar a tá sé.

Some say I'm foolish and more say I'm wise.
Being fond of the women I think is no crime.
The son of King David had ten hundred
 wives.
His wisdom is highly recorded.

I'll till up the garden and live at me ease.
Each woman and child can partake of the
 same.
If there's more in the cabin themselves they
 might blame.
Fágaimíd siúd mar a tá sé.

Now for the future I mean to be wise.
I'll send for the women that acted so kind
And marry them all on the morrow bye and
 bye
If the clergy agree to the bargain.

When I'm on me back and me soul is at
 peace
These women will crowd for to cry at me
 wake.
My sons and daughters will offer the prayer
To the Lord for the soul of their father.

This is in Colm O'Loughlin's *Irish Street Ballads* and it describes the story of some men from up North who were deported to Van Diemens Land for poaching to feed their families.

On a Monday morning early as me wandering steps did take me
Down by a farmer's station, his meadows and green lawn,
I heard great lamentation, the wee birds they were making,
Said, 'We'll have no more engagements
With the boys of Mullabawn.'

My pardon to you, ladies, I'll ask you this one favour.
I hope it is not treason on you I now must call.
I'm condoling late and early, me heart is nigh on breaking
All for a noble lady
That lives near Mullabawn.

Squire Jackson he's unequalled in honour or in favour.
He never turned a traitor nor betrayed the right of man,
But now we are in danger from a vile deceiving stranger
Who has ordered transportation
For the boys of Mullabawn.

With the heroes on the ocean I'm told the ship in motion
Stowed up in wild commotion as if the seas ran dry.
The trout and salmon gaping as the cuckoo left her station
Saying, 'Fare thee well to Erin
And the hill of Mullabawn.'

To end this lamentation we're all in consternation
None want for recreation until the days do dawn,
For without hesitation we are charged with combination
And sent for transportation
From the hills of Mullabawn.

Sacco and Vanzetti

40

From the singing of Woody Guthrie. Two Italians who went to the States at the turn of the century were executed in 1926 and given a pardon in 1976 on the fiftieth anniversary of their death. The American govenment admitted that Sacco and Vanzetti had been framed.

Oh say there, did you hear the news?
Sacco worked at trimming shoes.
Vanzetti was a travelling man, pushed his cart
Round with his hand.

Chorus
Two good men's a long time gone.
Sacco and Vanzetti are gone.
Two good men's a long time gone.
They left me here to sing this song.

Sacco was born across the sea
Somewhere over in Italy.
Vanzetti born of parents fine
Drank the best Italian wine.

Sacco sailed the sea one day,
Landed over in the Boston bay.
Vanzetti sailed the ocean blue,
Ended up in Boston too.

Chorus

Sacco was a family man,
Sacco's wife three children had.
Vanzetti was a dreaming man,
His books were always in his hand.

Sacco made his bread and butter
Being the factory's best shoe cutter.
Vanzetti worked both day and night,
Showed the people how to fight.

Chorus

I'll tell you if you ask me
About the pay-roll robbery.
Two clerks were shot in the shoe factory
On the streets of old Braintree.

I'll tell you the prosecutors' names:
Katman, Adams, Williams, Kane.
Them and the judge were the best of friends.
Did more tricks than circus clowns.

The judge he told his friends around
He'd put them rebels down.
Communist bastards was the name
The judge he gave these two fine men.

Chorus

Vanzetti docked in '98.
Slept along a dirty street.
Showed the people how to organise.
Now in the electric chair he dies.

All us people ought to be
Like Sacco and Vanzetti.
Every day find ways to fight
On the union side for the workers' rights.

Chorus

I ain't got time to tell the tale
'Cause the branch and the bulls are on my tail.
I won't forget these men who died
To show us people how to live.

All you people in Window Lane
Sing this song and sing it plain.
Everyody here tonight
Singing this song we'll get it right.

Chorus

My very first radio broadcast was on the BBC in 1967. On the same programme were Dominic Behan and The Ian Campbell Folk Group. Ian Campbell wrote this song and sang it on that broadcast and kindly gave it to me.

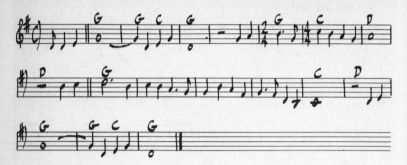

The sun is burning in the sky,
Strands of clouds go slowly driftin' by.
In the park, the dreamy bees are droning in the flowers among the trees
And the sun burns in the sky.

Now the sun is in the west
Little babes lay down to take their rest,
And the couples in the park are holding hands and waiting for the dark
And the sun is in the west.

Now the sun is sinking low.
Children playing know it's time to go.
High above a spot appears, a little blossom blooms and then draws near.
And the sun is sinking low.

Now the sun has come to earth
Shrouded in a mushroom cloud of death.
Death comes in a blinding flash of hellish heat and leaves a smear of ash
And the sun has come to earth.

Now the sun has disappeared
All that's left is darkness, pain and fear.
Twisted sightless wrecks of men go crawling on their knees and cry in pain
And the sun has disappeared.

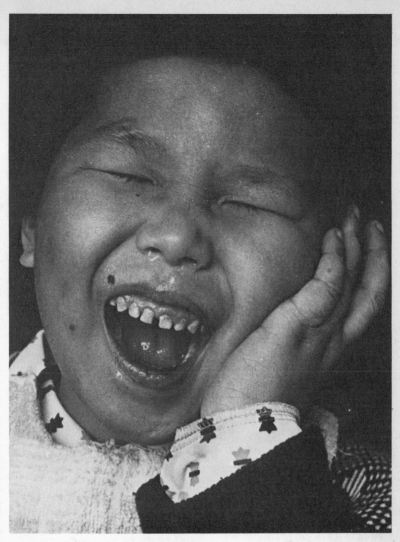

Cyril Byrne

I came across this on a broadsheet and added bits and pieces. The broadsheet was torn when I got it and I cannot remember what is original and what I added.

Patrick was a gentleman,
Came from decent people.
He built a church in Dublin town
And on it put a steeple.
His father was a Gallagher,
His mother was a Grady,
His aunt was an O'Shaughnessy,
His uncle was a Brady.
The Wicklow hills are very high
And so is the hill of Howth, sir,
But there's a hill much higher still,
Much higher than them both, sir.
On the top of this high hill
St Patrick preached his sermon
Which drove the frogs into the bogs
And banished all the vermin.
There's not a mile of Eireann's Isle
Where dirty vermin musters
But there he put his dear fore-foot
And murdered them in clusters.
The frogs went hop and the toads went
    pop
Slapdash into the water
And the snakes committed suicide
To save themselves from slaughter.

Nine hundred thousand reptiles blue
He charmed with sweet discourses
And dined on them in Killaloe
On soups and second courses.
Where blind worms crawling in the grass
Disgusted all the nation,
Right down to Hell with a holy spell
He changed their situation.
No wonder that them Irish lads
Should be so gay and risky.
Sure St Pat he taught them that
As well as making whiskey.
No wonder that the saint himself
Should understand distilling
For his mother kept a shebeen shop
In the town of Enniskillen.
Was I but so fortunate
As to be back in Munster,
I'd be bound that from that ground
I never more would once stir.
There St Patrick planted turf,
Cabbages and praties,
Pigs galore, mo grá, mo stór,
Altar boys and ladies.

Johnny Moynihan used to sing this song regularly and passed the words on to me.
Joe Heaney also sang it.

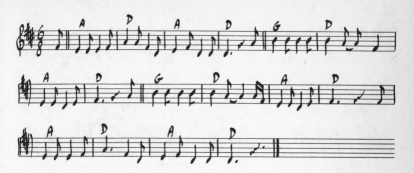

Come all you true born Irishmen wherever you may be,
I hope you'll pay attention and listen unto me.
I'll sing about a battle that took place the other day
Between a Russian sailor and Johnny Morrissey.

'Twas in Terra Del Fuego in South Americay
The Russian challenged Morrissey; these words to him did say,
'I hear you are a fighting man, you wear a belt I see.
Indeed I wish you would consent, to have a fight with me.'

Up spoke Johnny Morrissey with heart both brave and true,
'I am a valiant Irishman that never was subdued.
I can whack the Yankee, the Saxon bull or bear.
In honour of old Paddy's land the laurels I'll maintain.'

They shook hands and walked around the ring, commencing then to fight.
It filled each Irish heart with joy for to behold the sight.
The Russian floored Morrissey up to the eleventh round.
With Yankee, Saxon, Russian cheers, the valleys did resound.

But the Irish offered 10 to 1 that day upon the grass.
No sooner said than taken up, they then brought down the cash.
They parried away without delay up to the eighteenth round
When Morrissey received a blow which brought him to the ground.

Up to the thirty-second round 'twas fall and fall about,
Which caused the foreign tyrants to keep a sharp lookout.
The Russian called his seconds, to pour a glass of wine.
'Oh Begod,' says Johnny Morrissey, 'this battle will be mine.'

The thirty-third decided all, the Russian felt a smart,
When Morrissey, with a dreadful blow, struck the Russian on the heart.
They sent for the physician to open up a vein.
Says he, 'It is quite useless, he'll never fight again.'

Our hero conquered Thomson, the Yankee clipper too,
The Benica boy and shepherd, he nobly did subdue.
Let us fill a flowing glass and here's a health galore
To noble Johnny Morrissey who came from Templemore.

Fergus Bourke

One of the founder members of Sweeney's Men, Joe Dolan from Galway, wrote this song about the hardships of constant whiskey indulgence. The morning after becomes the Iron Behind the Velvet.

When I was young and handy in my
    prime
In taverns I would sit and bide my time.
It's there I met your company,
I'd sit and drink my fill.
It's there that you took hold of me,
I think you've got me still.

You're the foxy devil when you like.
You set my mind at ease and then you
    strike.
You set my head a reeling,
You make me shout and sing,
My memory flees, I get no ease,
Till I have a little drink.

You're the crafty rogue and that's for
    sure.
For your company there is no cure.
I've squandered all my money
And the best years of my life
All on your charms, in spite of harm,
In spite of peace and strife.

Whiskey in the morning or at night
Gives strength to sing and dance, to love
    and fight,
And so despite misfortune
I'll take you as you are —
The best of friends and enemies,
The best I've known by far.

Joe Dolan from Galway went to fight in the Six Day War and wrote this song to prove he'd been there. Don't know if he ever got there.

I'm a stranger here from Ireland's shore,
Been on the road six months or more;
Hikin', workin', travel in style,
I'm a vagabond from Ireland's Isle.
My sunburned thumb stuck up in the air,
Many's the lift from here to there;
Cars, buses, vans and trains
In the punishing heat, the snow and rain.

Chorus
Whack fol de diddle fel de diro deh
Whack fol de diddle fel de dero
Mrs Dolan your son he isn't workin'.

I came from Dublin to Jerusalem town.
Had a drink or two on the journey down.
At a railway station called Gare du Nord
I missed my train through garglin' hard.
Three days later in Napoli
On a Turkish boat I sailed to sea.
Slept in a hot hole down below,
Travellin' tourist class, you know.

Chorus

When the promised land came into sight
The customs man gave me a fright.
'How much money have you got with
    you, Joe?'
I bluffed and said, 'Fifty pounds or so.'
He said, 'Shalom,' I said, 'Good day.'
Grabbed my gear got fast away.
Down to the desert then I went,
Diggin' up history, livin' in a tent.

Chorus

It was in the Gulf of Aqaba
I met some Paddies and we had a fleadh,
Danced through the streets of Eilat Town,
Sang 'Sean South of Garryowen'.
I was travellin', I don't know.
You pack your gear get up and go.
Leave the crack for another bout,
Could damn well do with a pint of stout.

Chorus

Dunlavin is in West Wicklow not one hundred miles from where I was born.

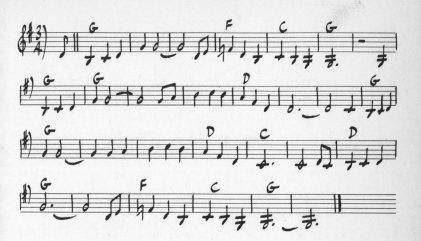

In the year of 1798,
A sorrowful tale the truth unto you I'll relate
Of thirty-six heroes, to the world they were left to be seen.
By false information they were shot on Dunlavin Green.

Bad luck to you, Saunders, their lives you sold away.
You said a parade would be held on that very day.
The drums they did rattle and the fifes they did sweetly play.
Surrounded we were and quietly marched away.

Quite easy they led us as prisoners through the town
To be shot on the plain; we then were forced to kneel down.
Such grief and such sorrow in one place it was ne'er before seen
As when the blood ran in streams down the dykes of Dunlavin Green.

There is young Andy Ryan has plenty of cause to complain,
Likewise the two Duffys who were shot down on the plain,
And young Mattie Farrell whose mother distracted will run
For the loss of her own darling boy, her eldest son.

Bad luck to you, Saunders, bad luck may you never shun,
That the widow's curse might melt you like snow in the sun.
The cries of those orphans whose murmurs you shall never screen,
For the loss of their own poor fathers who died on the Green.

Some of our boys to the hills they have run away.
More of them have been shot and some have run off to sea.
Michael Dwyer of the mountain has plenty of cause for the spleen
For the loss of his own dear comrades who died on the Green.

I cannot recall the source of this song.

You've heard of St Denis of France.
He never had much for to brag on.
You've heard of St George and his lance
Who killed d'old heathenish dragon.
The saints of the Welshmen and Scot
Are a couple of pitiful pipers
And might just as well go to pot
When compared to the patron of vipers:
St Patrick of Ireland, my dear.

He sailed to the Emerald Isle
On a lump of paving stone mounted.
He beat the steamboat by a mile
Which mighty good sailing was counted.
Says he, 'The salt water, I think,
Has made me unmerciful thirsty,
So bring me a flagon to drink
To wash down the mullygrups, burst ye,
Of drink that is fit for a saint.'

He preached then with wonderful force,
The ignorant natives a-teaching,
With wine washed down each discourse
For says he, 'I detest your dry preaching.'
The people in wonderment struck
At a pastor so pious and civil.
Exclaimed, 'We're for you, my oul buck,
And we'll heave our blind Gods to the
    devil
Who dwells in hot water below.'

This finished, our worshipful man
Went to visit an elegant fellow
Whose practice each cool afternoon
Was to get most delightfully mellow.
That day with a barrel of beer
He was drinking away with abandon.
Says Patrick, 'It's grand to be here.
I drank nothing to speak of since landing,
So give me a pull from your pot.'

He lifted the pewter in sport.
Believe me, I tell you it's not fable.
A gallon he drank from the quart
And left it back full on the table.
'A miracle!' everyone cried
And all took a pull on the Stingo.
They were mighty good hands at that
    trade
And they drank till they fell, yet by Jingo,
The pot it still frothed o'er the brim.

'Next day,' said the host, 'it's a fast
And I've nothin to eat but cold mutton.'
On Fridays who'd make such repast
Except an unmerciful glutton.
Said Pat, 'Stop this nonsense, I beg.
What you tell me is nothin but gammon.'
When the host brought down the lamb's
    leg
Pat ordered it turned into salmon,
And the leg most politely complied.

You've heard I suppose long ago
How the snakes, in a manner most antic,
He marched to the County Mayo
And ordered them all into the Atlantic.
Hence never use water to drink —
The people of Ireland determine
With mighty good reason, I think,
For Patrick has filled it with vermin
And snakes and such other things.

He was as fine a man
As you'd meet from Fairhead to
    Kilcrumper.
Though under the sod he is laid
Let's all drink his health in a bumper.
I wish he was here that my glass
He might by art magic replenish,
But since he is not why, alas,
My old song must come to a finish
Because all the drink it is gone.

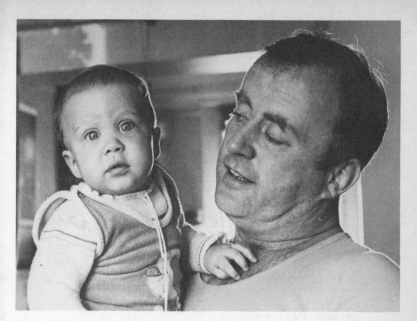

Pádraic and Christy Moore. Ann Egan

Written by Eamonn O'Doherty from Derry, this was a constant number in my repertoire until I sang it one night in Ballymurphy. Joe McCann was shot dead on the street while unarmed by British forces in April 1972 during the time that the Official IRA were still involved in military action. He was a great soldier.

Come all of you fine people, wherever you be,
I'll sing of a brave Belfast man
Who scorned the army's might, though they'd shoot him on sight.
And they shot down Joe McCann, Joe McCann,
They shot down Joe McCann.

He fought for the people of the Markets where he worked
In defence of the rights of man.
But the hired branch crew told the soldiers what to do,
And they shot down Joe McCann, Joe McCann,
They shot down Joe McCann.

In a Belfast bakery in the August of the year
When internment was imposed throughout the land
Six volunteers from Belfast held six hundred troops at bay
And their leader was Joe McCann, Joe McCann,
Their leader was Joe McCann.

He carried no gun so he started to run
To escape them as many the time before,
One bullet brought him down. As he lay on the ground,
They shot him ten times more, ten times more,
They shot him ten times more.

He fought for the rights of the people of this land,
The Protestant and Catholic working man.
He caused the bosses fear, for this they paid him dear
When they murdered brave Joe McCann, Joe McCann,
They murdered brave Joe McCann.

Written by Harvey Andrews from Birmingham about one of the four students shot dead by the National Guard at Kent State University during a protest against the Vietnam war.

The sun was hot and the air was heavy and the marching men came by.
You stood at the door and you watched them pass and you asked the reason why.
The sound of steel on their jackboot heel came pounding through your head.
Your reason is past, they've come at last, with the blessings of the dead.

Hey Sandy, hey Sandy, why are you the one?
All the years of growing up are wasted now and gone.
Did you see them turn, did you feel the burn of the bullets as they flew?
Hey Sandy, hey Sandy, just what did you do?

At the college square, they were standing there, with the flag and with the gun
And the whispered words as the young ones stirred, why are these things done?
And the air was still with the lonely thrill of now the hour is near
And the smell of sweat was better yet than the awful smell of fear.

The awful shout as you all ran out, why are these things done?
And you stood and stared yet no one cared for another campus bum.
Your songs are dead and your hymns instead are to the funeral pyre
And the words of youth, like love and truth, are just ashes on the fire.

Did you throw the stone at the men alone with their bayonets fixed for hire?
Did you think that they would kill no one, did you scream as they opened fire?
As the square ran red with your bloodstains spread and the darkness round you grew
Did you feel the pain, did you call the name of the man that you never knew?

Written by Sigerson Clifford. I first heard it in Birmingham sung by Mick Hipkiss.
Barr na Sráide was a street in Cahirciveen which was razed to the ground and all
its inhabitants scattered. Sung by Mick Hipkiss.

Oh the town it climbs the mountain and looks upon the sea.
At sleeping time or waking time, it's there I'd like to be.
To walk again those kindly streets, the place where life began,
With those boys of Barr na Sráide who hunted for the wren.

With cudgels stout they roamed about to hunt for the dreolín.
We searched for birds from every furze from Litir to Dooneen.
We danced for joy beneath the sky, life held no print or plan,
When the boys from Barr na Sráide went hunting for the wren.

And when the hills were bleeding and the rifles were aflame
To the rebel homes of Kerry the Saxon strangers came,
But the men who dared the Auxies and who fought the Black and Tan
Were those boys of Barr na Sráide who hunted for the wren.

But now they toil in foreign soil where they have made their way,
Deep in the heart of London town or over in Broadway,
And I am left to sing their deeds and praise them while I can,
Those boys of Barr na Sráide who hunted for the wren.

And here's a health to them tonight, wherever they may be:
By the groves of Carham river or the slopes of Bi na Tí
John Daly and Batt Andy and the Sheehans, Con and Dan,
And the boys of Barr na Sráide who hunted for the wren.

When the wheel of life runs out and peace comes over me,
Just take me back to that old town between the hills and sea.
I'll take my rest in those green fields, the place where life began,
With those boys of Barr na Sráide who hunted for the wren.

The only song I have recorded that I have never performed on stage since. I do believe I learned this song from Frank Harte from Chapelizod.

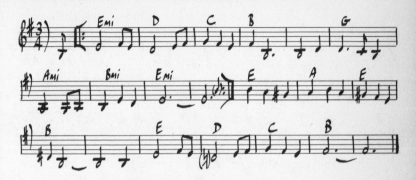

By Clyde's Bonny Banks as I sadly did wander
Among the pit heaps as evening drew nigh
I spied a fair maiden all dressed in deep mourning;
She was weeping and wailing with many a sigh.
I stepped up beside her and thus I addressed her,
'Pray tell me, fair maid, of your sorrow and pain.'
Oh sobbing and sighing at last she did answer.
'Johnny Murphy, kind sir, was my true lover's name.

'Twenty-one years of age, full of youth and good looking,
To work in the mines of high Blantyre he came.
The wedding was fixed all the guests were invited.
That calm summer's evening, my Johnny was slain.
The explosion was heard, all the women and children
With pale anxious faces they ran to the mine.
When the news was made known, all the hills rang with mourning.
Three hundred and ten young miners were slain.'

Now husbands and wives and sweethearts and brothers,
That Blantyre explosion you'll never forget.
And all you young miners that hear my sad story
Remember your comrades who lie at their rest.

Little Mother

I toured Norway in 1975 and one night I vaguely remember hearing these lyrics on somebody's record player. I have no idea who wrote it or where it came from. I doubt very much if this is the complete song but it is all I could recall from that night in Bergen.

Hey, Little Mother, what's in your bag?
Chocolates and sweets.

Hey, Mr Postman, what's in your bag?
A note from your beloved.

Hey, Mr Tailor, what's in your bag?
The finest wedding dress.

Hey, Mr Harvester, what's in your bag?
Solitude and death.

Eamonn O'Dwyer (Report)

As is often the case, an awful lot of stuff was put down to Pretty Boy Floyd, things that he did not do at all. Woody Guthrie wrote this song offering another view of Pretty Boy Floyd to the American public. Recently in Naas a traveller was charged with crimes which were committed while he was in Mountjoy jail — some things never change.

Come gather round me people and a story I will tell
About Pretty Boy Floyd the outlaw, Oklahoma knew him well.
In the town of Shawnee all on a Saturday afternoon,
With his wife beside him in the truck as into the town he rode.

There a deputy approached him in a manner very rude
Using vulgar language that his wife she overheard.
Pretty Boy grabbed a log chain and the deputy grabbed his gun.
In the fight that followed he laid the deputy down.

He took to the woods and mountains and the Canadian river shore.
Pretty Boy found a welcome at many a poor farmer's door.
He took to the woods and mountains and led a life of shame.
Every crime in Oklahoma was added to his name.

There is many a starving farmer the same old story told
How Pretty Boy paid their mortgage and saved their little homes.
More speak about a strange man who came to beg a meal
And underneath his napkin left a thousand dollar bill.

In the town of Shawnee all on a Christmas day
There came a car filled with groceries and a message that did say:
'You say I am an outlaw, you say I am a thief,
But here's a Christmas dinner for the children on relief.'

As round the world I travel I meet all kinds of men.
Some will rob you with a six gun, some with a fountain pen,
But as round the world I travel and round the world I roam
I've yet to see an outlaw drive a family from their home.

A farm labourer is hired at a hiring fair in Scotland up around Perthshire. In the period of the song the travelling man was considered to be a better catch than a farm labourer, which shows how things have changed from the point of view of the travelling people.

As I went out by Huntleigh town
One evening for to fee,
I met with Bogey O'Cairnee
And with him I did agree

To care for his two best horses
Or cart or harrow or plough
Or anything about farm work
That I very well should know.

Old Bogey had a daughter.
Her name was Isobel.
She's the lily of the valley
And the primrose of the dell.

And when she went out walking
She took me for her guide
Down by the Burn O'Cairnee
To watch the small fish glide.

And when three months was past and
gone
This girl she lost her bloom.
The red fell from her rosy cheeks
And her eyes began to swoon.

And when nine months were past and
gone
She bore to me a son
And I was straight sent for
To see what could be done.

I said that I would marry her
But that it would nae do.
'You're no a match for my boney wee
girl
And she's no match for you.'

Now she's married to a tinker lad
That comes from Huntleigh town.
He sells pots and pans and paraffin
lamps
And scours the country round.

Maybe she's had a better match.
Old Bogey can nae tell.
So fair well, ye lads o' Huntleigh town
And to Bogey's bonny belle.

The Crack Was Ninety in the Isle of Man

I learned this from Barney Rush in the Channel Islands at the same time as 'Nancy Spain'; about a visit Barney and his friends made to the Isle of Man in the late fifties.

Well weren't we the rare oul stock;
Spent the evenin' gettin' locked
Up in the Ace a Hearts
Where the high stools were engaging.
Over the Butt Bridge, down by the dock,
The boat she sailed at five o'clock.
'Hurry, boys, now,' said Whack,
'Or before we're there we'll all be back.'
Carry him if you can.
The crack was ninety in the Isle of Man.

Before we reached the Alexander Base
The ding dong we did surely raise.
In the bar of the ship we had great sport
As the boat she sailed out of the port.
Landed up in the Douglas Head.
Enquired for a vacant bed.
The dining room we soon got shown
By a decent woman up the road.
'Lads, ate it if you can.'
The crack was ninety in the Isle of Man.

Next morning we went for a ramble
    round;
Viewed the sights of Douglas Town.
Then we went for a mighty session
In a pub they call Dick Darbies.
We must have been drunk by half past
    three.
To sober up we went swimmin' in the
    sea.
Back to the digs for the spruce up
And while waitin' for the fry
We all drew up our plan.
The crack was ninety in the Isle of Man.

That night we went to the Texas Bar;
Came back down by horse and car.
Met Big Jim and all went in
To drink some wine in Yate's.
The Liverpool Judies it was said
Were all to be found in the Douglas Head.
McShane was there in his suit and shirt.
Them foreign girls he was tryin' to flirt
Sayin', 'Here, girls, I'm you man.'
The crack was ninety in the Isle of Man.

Whacker fancied his good looks.
On an Isle of Man woman he was struck
But a Liverpool lad was by her side
And he throwin' the jar into her.
Whacker thought he'd take a chance.
He asked the quare one out to dance.
Around the floor they stepped it out
And to Whack it was no bother.
Everythin' was goin' to plan.
The crack was ninety in the Isle of Man.

The Isle of Man woman fancied Whack.
Your man stood there till his mates came
    back.
Whack! they all whacked into Whack
And Whack was whacked out on his
    back.
The police force arrived as well;
Banjoed a couple of them as well.
Landed up in the Douglas jail
Until the Dublin boat did sail,
Deported every man.
The crack was ninety in the Isle of Man.

From the singing of Hamish Imlach of Motherwell in Scotland. There is a West Clare version which I have heard sung by Liam Weldon and even though the songs are dissimilar in melody the lyrics are similar.

Black is the colour of my true love's hair.
Her lips are like some roses fair.
She has the sweetest smile and the
    gentlest hands
And I love the ground whereon she
    stands.

I love my love and well she knows.
I love the ground whereon she goes.
I wish the day it soon would come
When she and I could be as one.

I go to the Clyde and I mourn and weep
For satisfied I ne'er can be.
I write her a letter, just a few short
    lines,
And suffer death a thousand times.

The Good Ship Kangaroo

From the singing of Elizabeth Cronin from Macroom in Co. Cork.

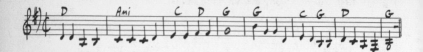

Once I was a waitin' man that lived at home at ease.
Now I am a mariner that ploughs the angry seas.
I always loved seafarin' life; I bid my love adieu.
I shipped as steward and cook, me boys, on board the Kangaroo.

Chorus
Oh I never thought she would prove false or either prove untrue
As we sailed away through Milford Bay on board the Kangaroo.

'Think of me, oh think of me,' she mournfully did say,
'When you are in a foreign land and I am far away.
Take this lucky trupenny bit, it'll make you bear in mind
That lovin' trustin' faithful heart you left in tears behind.'

'Cheer up, cheer up, my own true love. Don't weep so bitterly.'
She sobbed, she sighed, she choked, she cried and could not say goodbye.
'I won't be gone for very long, 'tis but a month or two.
When I will return again of course I'll visit you.'

Our ship it was homeward bound from many's the foreign shore
And many's the foreign present unto me love I bore.
I brought tortoises from Tenerife and toys from Timbuktu
A china rat, a Bengal cat and a Bombay cockatoo.

Paid off I sought her dwellin' on a street above the town
Where an ancient dame upon the line was hangin' out her gown.
'Where is me love?' 'She's vanished, sir, six months ago
With a smart young man that drives the van for Chaplin, Son and Co.'

Here's a health to dreams of married life, to soap suds and blue,
Heart's true love and patent starch and washin' soda too.
I'll go unto some foreign shore, no longer can I stay
And with some China hottentot I'll throw meself away.

Me love she is no foolish girl, her age it is two score.
Me love she is no spinster, she's been married twice before.
I cannot say it was her wealth that stole me heart away;
She's a washer in a laundry for one and nine a day.

The Pursuit of Farmer Michael Hayes

This is a song which I put together from about five or six different versions. Michael Hayes was a tenant farmer who was evicted by his landlord; in the course of the eviction he shot the bailiff dead and went on the run and finally escaped to America after leading a chase around Ireland for about three years.

I am a bold undaunted fox that never yet was trapped or caught.
Me rent, rates and taxes I was willin' for to pay.
I made me name in fine good land between Tipperary and Knocklong
Where me forefathers lived and died three thousand years ago.

I lived as happy as King Saul and loved me neighbours one and all,
Had no animosity for either friend or foe,
Then I was of late betrayed by one who was a fool I know.
He told me I should leave the place and show me face no more.

The day that he evicted me, it's then I knew that I should flee.
Late one night I took his life and left him lyin' low.
He fell victim to a shot, his agency was soon forgot.
From that day on they're searchin' for farmer Michael Hayes.

Soon there was a great lookout by land and sea myself to rout
From Dublin Quay to Belfast along the ragin' sea.
By telegraph they did insert a great reward for my arrest,
Me figure, size and form, me name without mistake.

They broke their brogues a thousand pairs this great reward for to obtain;
Still their search was all in vain for farmer Michael Hayes.
They searched Tipperary o'er and o'er, the cornfields near Galtymore;
They then went into Wexford town but did not long delay.

Through Ballyhale and Stranemore, they searched the woods as they went on.
It's they were hungry, wet and cold before the break of day.
You may roam the world both far and near but never such a tale you'll hear
Of a fox to get away so clear as I did from them hounds.

They searched the rocks, the gulfs, the quays, the ships, the liners in the bays,
The ferryboats and steamers as they were goin' to sea.
Around the coast they made a steer from Poolbeg lighthouse to Cape Clear,
Killarney town and sweet Tralee; they then crossed into Clare.

When they landed on the shore, they searched Kilrush from tip to toe.
They searched the baths at sweet Lisdoon, likewise Milltown Malbay.
Galway bein' a place of fame, they thought 'twas there I might remain,
Still their search was all in vain for I gave them all leg bail.

They searched the train at Oranmore as she was leavin' for Athlone,
Every wagon, car and coach they met along the road.
Connemara bein' remote, they thought 'twas there I might resort;
As they were gettin' weary they resolved to try Mayo.

In Ballaghaderreen they had to rest until the hounds they were refreshed.
They then went on to Westport and searched it high and low.
Through Castlebar they made a trot when they heard I was in Castlerock,
Still they were deluded where I lodged the night before.

In Swinford town as I lay down, I heard a dreadful cry of hounds
Which filled me with the notion to retaliate me chase.
Being weary from the road, I took a drink at half past four
Which filled me heart with strength and speed when the hounds were gettin' slow.

As the moon began to shine I thought I'd make a foreign clime,
Leave them all to search away for farmer Michael Hayes.
To Dublin town I made my way and then to Cobh and Americay;
Now I'm in the land of liberty, a fig for all my foes.

A ballad from John Reilly, though I was not able to make out all John's lyrics so I did write in certain verses myself. It is a very ancient ballad which is included in the Childe collection of ballads which is the greatest scholarly work about folk songs.

There was a Lord who lived in this land,
Being a lord of high degree.
He left his foot down in a ship's board
And swore strange countries that he
    would go see.

He travelled east and he travelled west,
He travelled north and south also,
Until he arrived into Turkey land.
There he was taken and bound in prison
Until his life it was weary.

Oh Turkey bold had one only daughter,
As fair a lady as the eye could see.
She stole the key to her Dado's harbour
And swore Lord Baker she would set free.

Singing, 'You have houses and you have
    linen,
And all Northumber belongs to thee.
What would you give to Turkey's
    daughter
If out of prison she'd set you free?'

Singing, 'I have houses and I have linen,
All Northumber belongs to me.
I would will them all to you, my darling,
If out of prison you'd set me free.'

She brought him down to her Dado's
    harbour
And filled for him was the ship of fame
And every toast that she did drink around
    him,
'I wish Lord Baker that you'd remain.'

They made a vow for seven years
And seven more to keep it strong
Saying, 'If you don't wed with no other
　woman,
I'm sure I'll wed with no other man.'

In seven years being past and over
And seven more they were rolling on
She's bundled all her gold and clothing
And swore Lord Baker she would go find.

She travelled east, and travelled west
Till she came to the palace of fame.
'Who's that, who's that?' cried the bold
　young porter.
'Who knocks so gently and can't get in?'

'Is this Lord Baker's palace?' replied the
　lady,
'Or is his lordship himself within?'
'This is Lord Baker's palace,' replied the
　porter,
'This very day took a new bride in.'

'Well ask him send me a cut of his
　wedding cake,
A glass of his wine that been e'er so
　strong,
And to remember a brave young lady
Who did release him in Turkey land.'

In goes, in goes, in goes the porter
And kneels down gently on his right
　knee.
'Rise up, rise up, my bold young porter,
What news, what news have you brought
　to me?'

Singing, 'I have news of a grand arrival,
As fair a lady as the eye could see
She is at the gate
Waiting for your charity.

'She wears a gold ring on every finger,
And on the middle one where she wears
　three,
She has more gold hung around her
　middle
Than would buy Northumber and family.

'She asked you send her a cut of your
　wedding cake
A glass of your wine, it been e'er so
　strong,
And to remember a brave young lady
Who did release you in Turkey land.'

He took his sword by the handle,
Cut the wedding cake in pieces three,
Singing 'Here's a piece for Turkey's
　daughter,
Here's a piece for the new bride and one
　for me.'

Down comes, down comes the new
　bride's mother.
'What will I do with my daughter dear?'
'Your daughter came with one bag of
　gold.
I'll avert her home love with thirty-three.'

And then Lord Baker ran to his darling.
Of twenty-one steps he made but three.
He put his arms around Turkey's
　daughter
And kissed his true love most tenderly.

I first heard this song at the second Carnsore Anti-Nuclear Power Show in 1979 sung by Jim Page.

They dropped the bomb in '45 to end the
world war.
No one had ever seen such a terrible sight
before.
The world looked on with eyes wide to see
where it might lead.
The politics of power they passed around the
seed.
It was a time to remember, we never can
forget
They were playin' Hiroshima Nagasaki
Russian roulette.

They arose like the saviours of our modern
human race
With radiation haloes that hung about their
face
With the key to the sure-cure, the treatment
of our ills,
A hot-shot of cobalt and a pocket full of pills,
Speaking always of the enemy who lurked
across the sea
While they crept in among us like a carrier
disease.

Deep down inside the bunkers of the concrete
and the lead,
Einstein's disciples working steadily ahead,
Making heavy metal power-plants to fire the
city lights.
All you can hear in the underground is the
humming through the night.
The walls of tight security circle all around
Where they spill out their poison and they
bury it in the ground.

Holed up in the harbours, hidden secretly
away,
Warheads and submarines, they await to
make their play.
The military masterminds improve on their
designs.
The soldiers get all doped up and stumble

through the lines.
The spills into the rivers get carried out by
the tide.
They call this security but we're not satisfied.

Our statesmen and leaders with their
politicians' pay,
Quick to heed the hand that feeds, they're
careful what they say.
They call out experts to assure us, to wave
their magic wands.
This is the power of the future and the future
marches on.
And they call in all their favours, all their
political gains,
While the spills fill the rivers and settle in the
plains.

They've caused the death of millions, that's
their stock in trade.
They will be afflicted by the fallout and that
they've made.
They've sealed their own inevitable doom
and it must surely come.
Not even the moons of Jupiter will be far
enough away to run
When this earth that they've assaulted begins
to turn around
And the unavoidable gravity sucks them to
the ground.

I know the minds behind them, they are
riddled full of holes,
Not to be trusted with their hands at the
controls.
Their eyesight it is twisted by the glory of
their careers,
The heaped praise of flattery is music to their
ears.
To listen to them talk about how it hasn't
happened yet's
Like playin' Hiroshima Nagasaki Russian
roulette.

Originally written for me by Phil Chevron, he had no way of contacting me so recorded it himself before he finally got around to giving it to me.

This graveyard hides a million secrets
And the trees know more than they can tell.
The ghosts of the saints and the scholars will haunt you
In heaven and in hell.

Rattled by the glimmer man, the boogie man, the holy man,
And livin' in the shadows, in the shadows of a gunman.
Rattled like the coppers in your greasy till,
Rattled until time stood still.

Look over your shoulder, hear the school bell ring.
Another day of made-to-measure history.
I don't care if your heroes have wings,
Your terrible beauty's been torn.

Chorus
Faithful departed, we fickle hearted,
As you are now so once were we.
Faithful departed, we the meek hearted,
With graces imparted bring flowers to thee.

The girls in the kips proclaim their love for you.
When you stumbled in they knew you had a shilling or two.
They cursed you on Sundays and holy days of abstinence
When you all stayed away.

When you slept there a naked light bulb hid your shame.
Your shadows on the wall, they took all the blame.
The Sacred Heart's picture, compassion in his eyes,
Drowned out the river of sighs.

Let the grass grow green over the brewery tonight.
It'll never come between the darkness and the light.
There is no pain that can't be eased
By the devil's holy water and the rosary beads.

Chorus

You're a history book I never could write,
Poetry in paralysis, too deep to recite.
Dress yourself, bless yourself, you've won the fight.
We're gonna celebrate tonight.

Maybe we'll even climb the pillar like you always meant to,
Watch the sun rise over the strand.
Close our eyes and we'll pretend
It could somehow be the same again.

I'll bury you upright so the sun doesn't blind you.
You won't have to gaze at the rain and the stars.
Sleep and dream of chapels and bars
And whiskey in the jar.

Final Chorus
Faithful departed, look what you've started;
An underdog's wounds aren't so easy to mend.
Faithful departed, there's no broken hearted
And no more tristesse in your world without end.

Written by Jack Warshaw when he came to visit Belfast in 1977 and regularly
updated, I learnt it from the singing of a group called the Men of No Property, now
called the People of No Property.

They call it the law; we call it apartheid, internment, conscription, partition and silence.
It's the law that they make to keep you and me where they think we belong.
They hide behind steel and bullet-proof glass, machine guns and spies,
And they tell us who suffer the tear gas and the torture that we're in the wrong.

Chorus
No time for love if they come in the morning,
No time to show tears or for fears in the morning,
No time for goodbye, no time to ask why,
And the sound of the siren's the cry of the morning.

They suffered the torture, they rotted in cells, went crazy, wrote letters and died.
The limits of pain they endured, but the loneliness got them instead
And the courts gave them justice as justice is given by well-mannered thugs.
Sometimes they fought for the will to survive, but more times they just wished they were dead.

Chorus

They took away young Francis Hughes and his cousin Tom McIlwee as well.
They came for Patsy O'Hara and Bobby Sands and some of his friends.
In Boston, Chicago, Saigon, Santiago, Warsaw and Belfast
And places that never make headlines, the list never ends.

Chorus

The boys in blue are only a few of the everyday cops on the beat,
The C.I.D., Branchmen, the Blacks and the Gilmores do their jobs as well;
Behind them the men who tap phones, take photos, programme computers and files
And the man who tells them when to come and take you to your cell.

Chorus

Come all you people who give to your sisters and brothers the will to fight on,
They say you can get used to a war, that doesn't mean that the war isn't on.
The fish need the sea to survive just like your people need you
And the death squad can only get through to them if first they can get through to you.

Chorus

Yes the sound of the siren's the cry of the morning,
Oh the sound of the siren's the cry of the morning.

Merrion Road riot following H-Block march prevented from reaching the British Embassy (18 July 1981). Eamonn O'Dwyer (Report)

Landlord

Written by Jim Page, this song is often heard played on record players in Rathmines and Ranelagh on Saturday mornings.

Here he comes, lookin' for the rent,
His greedy yellow eyes and his tongue all bent,
Padlocked pockets and bad luck nose
Sniffin' 'round my doorway and goin' through my clothes.
Oh how could you treat me so cold?
Got a mortgage on my body and the deeds of my soul.

I've a run-down room with a two-way roof.
That man's a thief, I've even got the proof.
He likes to take, he doesn't like to give.
I have to pay him rent just to have a place to live.
Hey you, I know you well;
You run a rock-and-roll tavern and a greasy hotel.
You misuse a lot of people. You're such a greedy man.
I have to put gloves on in case I touch your hand.
Oh how could you treat me so cold?
Got a mortgage on my body and the deeds of my soul.

You go sneakin' 'round windows to see what you can see.
You unlock doors where you've got no right to be.
Your legs are weak. You've been tellin' lies.
Some day somebody's gonna get wise.
You're gonna get evicted out in the street,
No food in your belly and no shoes on your feet.
You're gonna walk around from door to door
But nobody's gonna want to see you anymore.
Oh how could you treat me so cold?
Got a mortgage on my body and the deeds of my soul.

You're gonna wake up down here on the street,
Bricks and mortar lyin' 'round your feet.
Treat me cold now, cold as you please;
Come next winter the two of us will freeze.
Oh landlord,
How could you treat me so cold?

One night after a Hearts gig in the Baggot Inn, Dublin, John Gibbs the author of the song sent up an empty Major packet with this song written on the back of it. We were so taken with it that we started rehearsing it the same night and two years later found that it had passed into the tradition. Of all the songs I have ever done this and 'Only Our Rivers Run Free' were the songs that became part of the general Irish repertoire in a very quick time.

Once upon a time there was
Irish ways and Irish laws,
Villages of Irish blood
Waking to the morning,
Waking to the morning.

Then the Vikings came around,
Turned us up and turned us down,
Started building boats and towns.
They tried to change our living,
They tried to change our living.

Cromwell and his soldiers came,
Started centuries of shame,
But they could not make us turn.
We are a river flowing,
We're a river flowing.

Again, again the soldiers came,
Burnt our houses, stole our grain,
Shot the farmers in their fields,
Working for a living,
Working for a living.

Eight hundred years we have been down.
The secret of the water sound
Has kept the spirit of a man
Above the pain descending,
Above the pain descending.

Today the struggle carries on.
I wonder will I live so long
To see the gates being opened up
To a people and their freedom,
A people and their freedom.

Remember the Brave Ones

Written by Barry Moore.

Remember the brave ones with the blackened face
Diggin' the trenches for the human race.
Remember the brave ones with the sanded eyes
Storming the beach-head. Hear the battle cry,
Mow them down!

The European fields and the coastal sands
Ran wet and warm where warriors had spilled.
This Christian sacrifice must never happen again.
The search began to find a cleaner way to kill.

Remember the brave ones who flew the skies,
Dropping their gifts down on the passers-by.
Deliver to London and to Dresden Town.
Let the buildings and rubble be their sleeping gown.
Blow them up!

The European cities, European towns,
Ran wet and warm where peaceful people spilled.
This Christian sacrifice must never happen again.
The search began to find a cleaner way to kill.

Remember the brave ones when the button is down
In an office in Moscow or in Washington
And the faceless features of a child unborn
To a civilisation that wouldn't live to learn
To forget the brave ones and let them lie.
Let their death moans be a warning cry
Of a battle that burns up like a million suns,
Where there are no heroes and there are no brave ones.
Forget the brave ones.

All I Remember

Mick Hanly wrote this song and presented it to me one night in Cork as a possible for the Moving Hearts repertoire, which indeed it was.

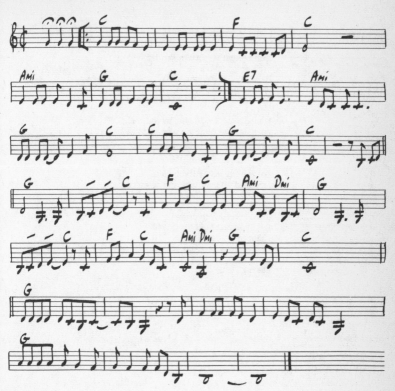

Lured by the rocking horse,
Sweets and bualadh bas,
Fifty wild boys to a room.
Sing lámh, lámh eile, the dish ran away
    with the spoon.
Black shoes and stockings for those who
    say don't.
Blue is the colour outside.
God made the world.
The snake tempted Eve and she died.
Wild Christian Brothers sharpening
    their leathers.
Learn it by heart, that's the rule.
All I remember is dreading September
    and school.

Chorus
And they made me for better or worse
The fool that I am or the wise man I'll be,
And they gave me their blessing or curse.
It wasn't their fault I was me. . .
Not the one that you see.

The priest in confession condemns my
    obsession
With thoughts that I do not invite.
I mumble and stutter,
He slams down the shutter,
Goodnight.
Stainless as steel,
Lord you know how I feel,
Someone shoot me while my soul is
    clear.
I don't think I'll last
But my vow to abstain was sincere.
Arch-confraternity men to the fight,
Raise up your banners on high;
Searching for grace,
Securing my place
When I die.

Chorus

God kept a very close eye on me.
Hung round my bed in the darkness
    He spied on me,
Found me in the long grass,
So often He died on me.
Ballrooms of romance in Salthill and
    Mallow,
I stood like John Wayne by the wall.
Lined up like cattle we wait to do battle
    and fall.
You can't wine and dine her in an old
    Morris Minor,
But ask her before it's too late.
I stepped on girls' toes and accepted
    rejection as my fate.
Drink was my saviour,
It made me much braver,
But I couldn't hold it too well.
I slipped on the coach
And it ruined my approach when I fell.

Chorus

Written by Don Laing and learned from the singing of Peggy Seeger.

The night hawk flies and the owl cries as we're driving down the road
Listening to the music, on the all night radio show.
The announcer comes on says, "If you've got ideas I'll file the patent for you.
What's an idea that's not in the store, makin' a buck or two?"

We drive to the town but the shutters are down and the night-restaurants closed.
It's the land of the free, they've booze and TV and there's tramps in the telephone booths.
The stars and the trees and the early spring breeze say forget what assassins have done,
Take the good soil in the palm of your hand and wait for tomorrow's sun.

It's a long way from the heartland to Santiago Bay
Where the good doctor lies with blood in his eyes and the bullets read USA.

A truck driver's wife leads a strange life driving down the road
Carrying the goods, all the copper and wood. That's what makes America great.
The dollars like swallows fly to the south where they know they've something to gain —
Allende is killed — the trucks are rolling again.

The night hawk flies, the owl cries as we're driving down the road.
The full moon reveals the houses and fields where good people do what they're told
A poet lies with coins in his eyes, there's no-one around him to mourn.
Who needs a poet who won't take commands, who'd rather make love than war?

Based on a poem by Pierce McLoughlin which I found in a republican songbook; I added some lyrics and wrote a melody.

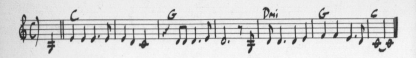

O'Hara, Hughes, McCreesh and Sands,
Doherty and Lynch,
McDonnell, Hurson, McIlwee, Devine.
Darkened years of winter have passed.
Summer waits for spring before it lives.
Blanket-clad and wasted, the winter has
   been long,
No gleam of hope a thoughtless nation
   gives.
In silence we walked through the streets
As one by one our hunger strikers died.

O'Hara, Hughes, McCreesh and Sands,
Doherty and Lynch,
McDonnell, Hurson, McIlwee, Devine.
Their memory is forever in my mind,
Pictures of their faces in my eyes.
My sorrow and grief will not subside
And my love for them I will not disguise.
In silence we walked through the streets
As one by one our hunger strikers died.

O'Hara, Hughes, McCreesh and Sands,
Doherty and Lynch,
McDonnell, Hurson, McIlwee, Devine.

Written by a republican from Lancashire who sent me the song only days after
Bobby Sands died.

How many more must die now, how many must we lose
Before the island people their own destiny can choose?
From immortal Robert Emmet to Bobby Sands MP,
Who was given 30,000 votes while in captivity.

No more he'll hear the lark's sweet notes upon the Ulster air
Or gaze upon the snowflake pure to calm his deep despair.
Before he went on hunger strike young Bobby did compose
The rhythm of time, the weeping winds and the sleeping rose.

Chorus
He was a poet and a soldier, he died courageously,
And we gave him 30,000 votes while in captivity.

Thomas Ashe gave everything in 1917;
The Lord Mayor of Cork McSweeney died his freedom to obtain.
Never a one of all our dead died more courageously than young
Bobby Sands from Twinbrook, the people's own MP.

Forever we'll remember him, that man who died in pain
That his country North and South might be united once again.
To mourn him is to organise and build a movement strong
With ballot box and armalite, with music and with song.

Chorus

The Plane Crash at Los Gatos

This song was written by Woody Guthrie to draw attention to a plane load of fruit pickers which had crashed on the way back to Mexico. These were people who had entered California illegally to pick fruit and then when the harvest was over were sent back home.

The crops are all in, they need us no longer.
The oranges are stacked in the creosote dumps.
They're driving us back to the Mexican border.
It takes all our money to go back again.

Chorus
Goodbye to my friends,
Goodbye, Rosalita.
Adios, mes amigos
Jesus y Maria.
You won't have a name
When you fly the big aeroplane,
All they will call you
Will be deportee.

My father's own father did wade through the Rio.
You took all the money he made in his life.
My sisters and brothers they worked in your fruit fields,
Rode on your trucks, till they laid down and died.

Chorus

Some of us are illegal, and all are not wanted;
Our work contracts out, we must move on
The six hundred miles to the Mexican border.
They drive us like outlaws, like rustlers, like thieves.

Chorus

Our sky plane caught fire o'er the Los Gatos canyon.
Like a fireball it fell to the ground.
Who are those friends lying there like dead leaves?
The radio said they were just deportees.

Chorus

We died on your hills, and we died in your valleys,
We died on your mountains, and we died in your plains,
We died 'neath your trees and we died 'neath your bushes.
Both sides of your border we died just the same.

Chorus

I have not been able to track down the author of this song but obviously it is about a young man from Ballina who gave his life on hunger strike in 1974 and the song says everything.

Take me home to Mayo
Back across the sea.
Take me home to Mayo
Where once I ran so free.
Take me home to Mayo
And let my body lie
Home in Mayo
Beneath the western sky.

My name is Michael Gaughan,
From Ballina I came.
I saw my people suffering,
I swore to break the chains.
I took the boat to England
Prepared to fight or die
Far away from Mayo
Beneath the western sky.

My body cold and hungry
In Parkhurst Jail I lie.
In my fight for freedom
On hunger strike I'll die.
I have one last request to make
I hope you'll not deny:
Take my body back to Mayo
Beneath the western sky.

Take me home to Mayo
Back across the sea.
Take me home to Mayo
Where once I ran so free.
Take me home to Mayo
And let my body lie
Home again in Mayo
Beneath the western sky.

This song was written by Joe Mulhearn from Derry and was in the repertoire of The Men of No Property.

As I was climbing into bed
At me poor granny's side
I looked out the window:
The Brits had arrived.
The house was surrounded;
They smashed the front door in.
They've come to take away
The lid of me granny's bin.

Well she opened up her window
And she clambered down the spout.
Soon her bin was rattling
To call the neighbours out.
She took out her whistle
And blew away like hell
And soon we heard an echo
As the neighbours blew as well.

Chorus
With a Scream, Bang, Shout,
Rattle up a din.
Let the army know, me Girls,
The Brits is comin' in.
Now rattle up your bin lid.
Beat the message out,
Get your head down.
Whistle, Bang, Shout!

A Tommy came right upstairs
A rifle in his hand.
She kicked him with her button boots
As down the hall she ran.
Up came another one
His medal for to win
But all he got right on the gob
Was the lid of me granny's bin.

The music rose like thunder
As the bins and whistles played.
The enemy soon retreated,
They knew they'd overstayed.
It wasn't made of silver,
It wasn't made of tin,
But once again it saved us all
The lid of me granny's bin.

Chorus

The English have the telly,
The radio and press;
To all communications
They've always had access.
But from Pettigo to Bellaghy
From the Bone to Castlefin,
The only way to spread the news
Is rattle your granny's bin.

Chorus

I wrote this song for the Hughes family from Bellaghy whose son Francis died on hunger strike on 12 May 1981.

As I walked through the Glenshane Pass I heard a young girl mourn.
'The boy from Tamlaghtduff,' she cried, 'is two years dead and gone.
How my heart is torn apart this young man to lose.
Oh I'll never see the likes again of my young Francis Hughes.

'For many years his exploits were a thorn in England's side.
The hills and glens became his home, there he used to hide.
Once when they surrounded him he quietly slipped away,
Like a fox he went to ground and kept the dogs at bay.

'Moving round the countryside he often made the news
But they could never lay their hands on my brave Francis Hughes.
Finally they wounded him and captured him at last.
From the countryside he loved, they took him to Belfast.

'Oh from Musgrave Park to Crumlin Road and then to an H-Block cell,
He went straight on the blanket then on hunger strike as well.
His will to win they could never break, no matter what they tried.
He fought them every day he lived and he fought them as he died.'

As I walked through the Glenshane Pass I heard a young girl mourn.
'The boy from Tamaghtduff,' she cried, 'is two years dead and gone.
Oh my heart is torn apart this brave man to lose.
I'll never see the likes again of my brave Francis Hughes.'

This was written by Ger Costello from Shannon in Co. Clare whose father wrote 'Sean South of Garryowen'. Ger was lead singer with a band called The Outfit who played support to Moving Hearts on many occasions. He's one of the most promising songwriters in the country.

'Look at the dying soldier,'
I heard them whisper
And then I saw the blood come through my shirt.
Am I going to die here?
I don't want to die here.
Someone come and pick me from the dirt.
I don't want to die here,
Don't let me die here, oh no.

My hands get colder,
My thoughts grow weaker.
This must be the way it is.
Stop the shooting,
Don't you see I'm dying,
Someone come and say a prayer.
I don't want to die here,
Please don't let me die here, oh no.

My eyes are closing.
I see someone coming
But he turns his back and runs away.
They've stopped shooting,
It's started raining,
Jesus this must be the way.
I don't want to die here,
Don't let me die here, oh no.
I don't want to die here,
Please don't let me die here, oh no, oh. . .

I want to go back home where my friends are,
I want to go on living there. . .
I want to go back home where my friends are,
I want to go on living there. . .
I want to go back home where my friends are,
I want to go on living there. . .
I want to go back home where my friends are,
I want to go on living there. . .

McIlhatton was a well known man in the Glens of Antrim where he played fine music and was known to dispense fine drink. The song was written by Bobby Sands in the H-Blocks and was given to me by Colm Scullion of Bellaghy who spent many years in the H-Blocks with Bobby.

In Glenravels Glen there lives a man who some would call a God
For he could cure the dead or take your life and his price was thirty bob.
Come winter, summer, frost all over, a jig in spring and the breeze,
In the dead of night a man steps by — McIlhatton, if you please.

Chorus

'McIlhatton,' you blurt. 'We need you,' cry a million shakin' men.
'Where are your sacks of barley? Will your likes be seen again?
Here's a jig to the man and a reel to the drop and a swing to the girls he loves,
May your fiddle play and poitín cheer your company up above.'

There's a wisp of smoke to the south of the Glen and the poitín is on the air,
The birds in the burrows and the rabbits in the sky and there's drunkards everywhere.
At Skerries rock the fox is out and by god he's chasing the hounds
And the only thing in dacent shape is buried beneath the ground.

Chorus

Oh McIlhatton

In McIlhatton's house the fairies are out and dancing on the hobs,
The goat's collapsed, the dog's run away and there's salmon down the bogs.
He has a million gallons of wash and the peelers are on the Glen
But they'll never catch McIlhatton cause he'll never come back again.

Chorus

Written by Brian Moore of Belfast who also performed with The Men of No Property.

Will you come and listen to the story going round
How Our Lord and Jesse James rode into Belfast town.
They stopped for a drink, stopped for a meal;
Drinking whiskey, drinking wine, they were feeling mighty fine
As they rode into Belfast through the hills of Ligoniel.

And not a word was spoken as they travelled on their way
Until they came to the Falls Road and Jesse he did say,
'God, I haven't felt so good since I robbed the Glendale train.'
Our Lord he raised his head, turned to Jesse and he said,
'I never thought I'd see the likes of Calvary again.'

They rode past the burnt out motorcars and the tangle of babed wire
In the city built upon the swamp and baptised in fire.
Our Lord was going to bless the place but a bullet grazed his hand.
As the blood came trickling red he turned to Jesse and he said,
'It's just that oul stigmata; it's infectious in this land.'

Our Lord was up on a donkey, Jesse James was riding a mare
And they rode past the army tanks and never showed a care.
Jesse on his fiddle played 'The Victory at the Boyne'.
Jesus put his bozouki down, turned to Jesse with a frown,
'I don't think you should play that tune when we're passing through Ardoyne.'

And when they came to Ballymurphy Des Wilson up and said,
'If you give us back our freedom you can keep your fish and bread.'
Jesse walked among the crowd to see what he could see.
His possessions they were few so he picked a pocket or two.
He was serving his apprenticeship with the SDLP.

On the top of Divis mountain there stands a lonely tree
And children passing by there, they stop and bend a knee,
And men with hidden guns make a silent vow
That the riots will stop the day that the soldiers go away,
Leave our Lord on the cross and Jesse hanging from the bough.

Back Home in Derry

Written by Bobby Sands for his comrades from Derry who were in the H-Blocks.
He performed this song at the nightly concerts they used to have in the Blocks,
singing it out through the keyhole to his Derry comrades.

In 1803 we sailed out to sea
Out from the sweet town of Derry
For Australia bound if we didn't all
  drown
And the marks of our fetters we carried.

In the rusty iron chains we sighed for our
  wains
As our good wives we left in sorrow.
As the mainsails unfurled our curses we
  hurled
On the English and thoughts of
  tomorrow.

Chorus

Oh Oh Oh Oh I wish I was back home in
  Derry.
Oh Oh Oh Oh I wish I was back home in
  Derry.

I cursed them to hell as our bow fought
  the swell,
Our ship danced like a moth in the
  firelights.
White horses rode high as the devil
  passed by
Taking souls to Hades by twilight.

Five weeks out to sea we were now
  forty-three
Our comrades we buried each morning.
In our own slime we were lost in a time,
Endless night without dawning.

Chorus

Van Diemen's land is a hell for a man
To live out his life in slavery,
Where the climate is raw and the gun
  makes the law,
Neiher wind nor rain cares for bravery.

Twenty years have gone by and I've
  ended me bond
And comrades' ghosts are behind me.
A rebel I came and I'll die the same.
On the cold winds of night you will find
  me.

Chorus

Written by Christy Hennessy from Tralee in Co. Kerry who has lived in London for many years. I find it humorous but also sometimes a little sad.

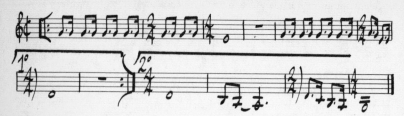

Don't forget your shovel if you want to go to work.
Oh don't forget your shovel if you want to go to work.
Don't forget your shovel if you want to go to work
Or you'll end up where you came from like the rest of us — digging —
Ow di diddle do.

And don't forget your shoes and socks and shirt and tie and all.
Don't forget your shoes and socks and shirt and tie and all.
Mr Murphy's afraid you'll make a claim if you take a fall.
How's it goin' — Not too bad —
Ow di diddle do.

And we want to go to heaven but we're always diggin' holes.
We want to go to heaven but we're always diggin' holes.
Yea we want to go to heaven but we're always diggin' holes.
Well there's one thing you can say — we know where we are going.
Any chance of a start — No — ok —
Oh di diddle do.

And if you want to do it — don't you do it agin the wall.
If you want to do it — don't you do it agin the wall.
Never see a toilet on a building site at all.

Mind your sandwiches.

Enoch Powell will give us a job, diggin' our way to Annascaul.
Enoch Powell will give us a job, diggin' our way to Annascaul.
Enoch Powell will give us a job, diggin' our way to Annascaul.
And when we're finished diggin' there he'll close the hole and all.

Now there's six thousand five hundred and fifty-nine Paddies over there in London
All trying to dig their way back to Annascaul.
And very few of them boys is going to get back at all — I think that's terrible.

Don't forget your shovel if you want to go to work.
Oh don't forget your shovel if you want to go to work.
Oh don't forget your shovel if you want to go to work.
Or you'll end up where you came from like the rest of us — diggin' diggin' diggin' —
Dow di diddle doh.

Written by Barry Moore as part of a campaign against this piece of legislation which prohibits Sinn Fein's elected representatives from putting forward their views on radio and TV.

Who are they to decide what we should hear?
Who are they to decide what we should see?
What do they think we can't comprehend here?
What do they fear that our reaction might be, might be?

Chorus
Section 31 on the TV,
Section 31 on the radio,
Section 31 is like a blindfold.
Section 31 makes me feel cold, feel cold.

The pounding of the footsteps in the early morning light,

Another family waking to an awful deadly fright.
There's a body on the pavement with a bullet to the jaw,
A thirteen-year-old victim of plastic bullet law.

The silence in my ears, the darkness in my eyes,
Heightens the fears, deafens the cries
Of another brother taken in another act of hate,
A family preparing for another dreadful wait.

Chorus

Written originally for Peggy O'Hara from Derry whose son Patsy died on the 21 May 1981 after sixty-one days on hunger strike, and I subsequently dedicated it to the families of all hunger strikers. In most cases it's the families or the wives of the hunger strikers that have to take the final decision and have to allow their sons go ahead with their sacrifice once they've lapsed into unconsciousness.

The time has come to part, my love,
I must go away.
I leave you now, my darling girl,
No longer can I stay.

My heart like yours is breaking,
Together we'll prove strong.
The road I take will show the world
The suffering that goes on.

The gentle clasp that holds my hand
Must loosen and let go.
Please help me through the door
Though instinct tells you no.

Our vow it is eternal
And will bring you dreadful pain,
But if our demands aren't recognised,
Don't call me back again.

How their sorrow touched us all
In those final days.
When it was time she held the door
And touched his sallow face.

The flame he lit by leaving
Is still burning strong.
By the light it's plain to see
The suffering still goes on.

The time has come to part, my love,
I must go away.
I leave you now, my darling girl,
No longer can I stay.

Eamonn O'Dwyer (Report)

I dedicate this song to the various Ministers of Justice who kept Nicky Kelly under lock and key for four years despite a general awareness around the country that he was completely innocent.

As I walked past Portlaoise Prison,
'I'm innocent,' a voice was heard to say.
'My frame-up is almost completed.
My people all look the other way.'

Seven years ago his torture started,
A forced confession he was made to sign.
Young Irish men specially trained and
chosen
Were on the heavy gang that made him
run the line.

Others in the Bridewell heard him
screaming.
Even prison doctors could see
His injuries were not self-inflicted.
Those who tipped the scales did not
agree.

Chorus

Give the Wicklow Boy his freedom,
Give him back his liberty,
Or are we going to leave him in chains
While those who framed him hold the
key?

Deprived of human rights by his own
people,
Sickened by injustice he jumped bail,
In the Appalachian Mountains found a
welcome
Till his co-accused were both released
from jail.

He came back home expecting to get
justice,
Special Branch took him from the plane.
For five years we've deprived him of his
freedom.
The guilty jeer the innocent again.

Chorus

The People versus Kelly was the title
Of the farce we staged at his appeal.
Puppets in well rehearsed collusion,
I often wonder how these men must feel.

As I walked past Portlaoise Prison
Through concrete and steel a whisper
came,
'My frame-up is almost completed.
I'm innocent, Nicky Kelly is my name.'

Chorus

Nicky Kelly, three days after his release from Portlaoise Prison, meets Christy Moore at the Wexford Inn, Dublin (20 July 1984). Derek Speirs (Report)

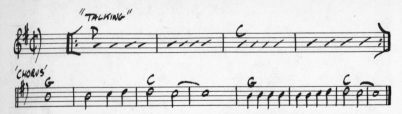

Lisdoonvarna

In 1983 I had the daunting task of having to go on before Rory Gallagher at the Lisdoonvarna festival. I wrote this song to aid me and I've more or less kept the song since then and added bits and pieces here and there and shaped and re-shaped it. In memory of six glorious years in Clare.

How's it goin', everybody,
From Cork, New York, Dundalk,
 Gortahork and Glenamaddy?
Here we are in the County Clare,
It's a long long way from here to there.
There's the Burren and the Cliffs of
 Moher,
The Tulla and the Kilfenora,
Miko Russell, Dr Bill,
Willy Clancy, Noel Hill,
Flutes and fiddles everywhere.
If it's music you want
Then go to Clare.

Chorus

Oh Lisdoonvarna, Lisdoon, Lisdoon,
 Lisdoon, Lisdoonvarna.

Everybody needs a break,
Climb a mountain, jump in a lake.
Some head off to exotic places,
Others go to the Galway races.
Mattie goes to the South of France,
Jim to the dogs, Peter to the dance.
A cousin of mine goes potholin',
A cousin of hers loves Joe Dolan.
As the summer comes around each year
We go there and they come here.
Some head off to Frijiliana
But I always go to Lisdoonvarna.

Chorus

I always leave on a Thursday night
With me tent and groundsheet rolled up
 tight.
I always like to hit Lisdoon
In or around a Friday afternoon.
This gives me time to get me gear
 together,
I don't need to worry about the weather.
Ramble in for a pint of stout,
You'd never know who'd be hangin'
 about.

Look there's a Dutchman playin' a
 mandolin
And a German lookin' for Liam Óg
 O'Floinn.
There's Adam, Bono and Garrett
 FitzGerald
Gettin' their photo taken for the **Sunday
 World**.
And there's Finbar, Charlie and Jim Hand
And they're drinkin' pints to bate the
 band.
Isn't it grand.

Chorus

The multitudes they flocked in throngs
To hear the music and the songs
On motorbikes and Hiace vans
With bottles, barrels, flagons, cans,
Mighty crack and loads of frolics,
Pioneers and alcoholics,
PLAC, SPUC and the FCA,
Free Nicky Kelly and the IRA,
Hairy chests and milk white thighs,
Mickey dodgers in disguise,
McGraths, O'Briens, Pippins, Cox's,
Massage parlours in horse boxes,
Amhráns, bodhráns, amadáns,
Arab sheikhs, Hindu sikhs, Jesus freaks,
RTE makin' tapes, takin' breaks, throwin'
 shapes.
This is heaven, this is hell.
Who cares? Who can tell?
Anyone for the last few choc ices?

Chorus

A 747 for Jackson Browne,
A special runway to get him down.
Before the Chieftains began to play
Seven creamy pints came out on a tray.
Sean Cannon did the backstage cookin',
Shergar was ridden by Lord Lucan.
Clannad playin' 'Harry's Game',

Christy singin' 'Nancy Spain'.
Mary O'Hara and Brush Shields
Together singin' 'The Four Green Fields'.
Van the Man and Emmy Lou,
Movin' Hearts and Planxty too.

Chorus

Everybody needs a break,
Climb a mountain, jump in lake.

Oliver J. Flanagan goes swimmin' in the
  Holy Sea,
Sean Doherty goes down for the Rose of
  Tralee,
But I like my music in the open air
So every summer I go to Clare.
Woodstock, Knock nor the Feast of Cana
Could hold a match to Lisdoonvarna.

Chorus

Christy Moore at Lisdoonvarna, 1983. Colm Henry

111

I wrote this song in Spain in 1983 in memory of the many Irish men who fought in Spain during the Spanish civil war. They went out under Frank Ryan to oppose the rising fascist tide and many of them never returned.

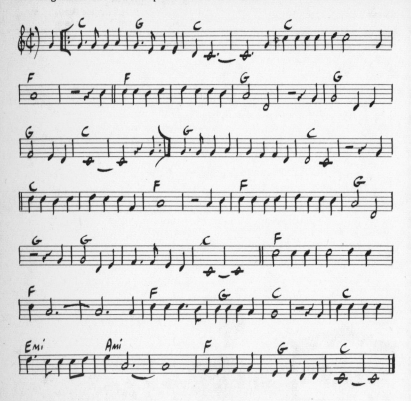

Ten years before I saw the light of morning
A comradeship of heroes was laid.
From every corner of the world came sailing
The Fifteenth International Brigade.

They came to stand beside the Spanish people,
To try and stem the rising Fascist tide.
Franco's allies were the powerful and wealthy,
Frank Ryan's men came from the other side.

Even the olives were bleeding
As the battle for Madrid it thundered on.
Truth and love against the force of evil,
Brotherhood against the Fascist clan.

Vive La Quince Brigada!
"No Paseran" the pledge that made them fight.
"Adelante" was the cry around the hillside.
Let us all remember them tonight.

Bob Hillard was a Church of Ireland pastor;
From Killarney across the Pyrenees he came.
From Derry came a brave young Christian Brother.
Side by side they fought and died in Spain.

Tommy Woods, aged seventeen, died in Cordoba.
With Na Fianna he learned to hold his gun.
From Dublin to the Villa del Rio
Where he fought and died beneath the Spanish sun.

Many Irishmen heard the call of Franco,
Joined Hitler and Mussolini too.
Propaganda from the pulpit and newspapers
Helped O'Duffy to enlist his crew.

The word came from Maynooth: 'Support the Fascists.'
The men of cloth failed yet again
When the bishops blessed the blueshirts in Dun Laoghaire
As they sailed beneath the swastika to Spain.

This song is a tribute to Frank Ryan,
Kit Conway and Dinny Coady too,
Peter Daly, Charlie Regan and Hugh Bonar.
Though many died I can but name a few:

Danny Doyle, Blaser-Brown and Charlie Donnelly,
Liam Tumilson and Jim Straney from the Falls,
Jack Nalty, Tommy Patton and Frank Conroy,
Jim Foley, Tony Fox and Dick O'Neill.

The clergy at Salamanca give the Fascist salute. From **Frank Ryan** by Sean Cronin (Academy Press)

Written by my brother Barry, based on the famine years when so many hundreds of thousands emigrated to America, leaving behind millions who died of hunger.

Chorus
In the city of Chicago
As the evening shadows fall
There are people dreaming
Of the hills of Donegal.

Eighteen forty-seven
Was the year it all began,
Deadly pains of hunger
Drove a million from the land.
They journeyed not for glory,
Their motive was not greed,
A voyage of survival
Across the stormy sea.

Chorus

Some of them knew fortune
Some of them knew fame,
More of them knew hardship
And died upon the plain.
They spread throughout the nation,
They rode the railroad cars,
Brought their songs and music
To ease their lonely hearts.

Chorus

Ride On

Written by Jimmy McCarthy from Cork.

True you ride the finest horse I've ever seen,
Standing 16 1" or 2" with eyes wild and green,
And you ride the horse so well, hands light to the touch.
I could never go with you no matter how I wanted to.

Chorus
Ride on, see you, I could never go with you,
No matter how I wanted to.

When you ride into the night without a trace behind,
Run your claw along my gut one last time;
I turn to face an empty space where once you used to lie
And look for a smile to light the night through a teardrop in my eye.

Chorus

Written by Johnny Duhan and given to me about three years ago. He has recorded it on his album, 'Current Affairs'.

A girl cries in the early morning,
Woken by the sound of a gun.
She knows somewhere somebody's
    dying,
Bleeding by the rising sun.
Outside the window of her cabana
The shadows are full of her fear.
She knows her lover is out there
    somewhere,
He's been fighting now for a year
To heal the soul of El Salvador.

The moon like a skull is over the country,
The sky to the east is blood-red.
A general wakes up and takes his coffee
While he sits on his bed.
Outside the barracks the soldiers are
    marching back
With their guns in their hands;
The general goes out, salutes his army
And issues new commands:
He makes the guns roar in El Salvador.

Bells ring out in a chapel steeple,
A priest prepares to say mass;
A sad congregation come tired
    and hungry
To pray that their troubles will pass.
Meanwhile the sun rises over the dusty
    streets
Where the bodies are found.
Flies and mosquitoes are drinking from
    pools of blood
Where the crowd gathers round.
They cry for the soul of El Salvador.

Out on the rancho the rich man's
    preparing
To go for his morning ride.
They've saddled his horse out in the
    corral,
He walks out full of pride.
He looks like a cowboy from one of
    the movies
A president made in the past.
Peasants in rags stand back for El Rico:
They know that he gallops real fast
Over the soul of El Salvador.

Written by Gerry Murray from Charlestown and dedicated to the memory of John Lennon who in his day wrote two songs for the Irish people.

The least we can do
Is make the world a better place,
Not just for a few
But all the human race,
To end wars and quarrels,
Make John Lennon's dream come true,
To build a new set of morals.
It's the least we can do.

Show some love and compassion
When people are feelin' low.
Make it not just a fashion
That may come and go.
Bring an end to oppression
'Cos it imprisons the truth
And be free with our expression.
It's the least we can do.

So follow his rainbow
Deep into the evenin' sun,
And pray that its colours
Will together blend as one.
Seek and we may find
The dream he loved to pursue,
A peace for all mankind.
It's the least we can do.

I first heard this many years ago and was recently reminded of it when out of the blue my five-year-old daughter Juno started singing it. I decided that maybe this was some kind of omen. I decided to learn it and start doing it myself. Written by Ron Hynes from Nova Scotia.

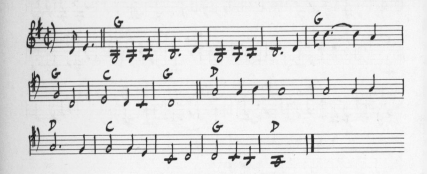

'Sonny, don't go away, I'm here all alone,
Your daddy's a sailor, never comes home.
Nights are so long, silence goes on,
I'm feelin' so tired and not all that strong.'

Sonny lives on a farm in a wide open space.
'Take off your shoes, son, stay out of the race,
Lay down your head by the soft river bed.'
Sonny always remembers the words his mammy said. .

Sonny works on the land though he's barely a man.
There's not much to do, he does just what he can.
He sits at the window of his room by the stairs,
He watches the waves gently wash on the pier.

Many years have passed on, Sonny's old and alone.
His daddy the sailor never came home.
Sometimes he wonders what his life might have been
But from the grave mammy still haunts his dreams.

Written by Tim Doc Whelan from Suncroft, close to Carnsore Point, who gave me this song at the first anti-nuclear festival in 1978.

Well me name is Nuke Power, a terror am I,
I can cause such destruction on land, sea or sky.
Your Minister tells you I'll do you no harm
If he locks me up in his house down in Carne.

Chorus
Toora loo, toora lay,
I can cripple and maim and cause death and decay.

He'll have me well guarded by night and by day
With soldiers on land and with sailors at sea;
But no one can tame me, I'll be restless I warn,
If he tries to lock me in his house down in Carne.

Chorus

Such a beautiful country I see all around
Where people and flowers and fishes abound.
I'll change that whole scene in ten seconds I warn
If he tries to lock me in his house down in Carne.

Chorus

I'll poison your children, I'll strangle your dog,
I'll kill every creature on land, sea and bog.
I'll devastate Ireland from Killarney to Larne
If he tries to lock me in his house down in Carne.

Chorus

Now I have three comrades called wind, rain and sun.
Very powerful are they and also they're great fun.
Treat them with respect and they'll do you no harm.
They'll work for you free every day down in Carne.

Chorus

Now to all you fine people, I make this strong plea.
Go tell your Minister to let me go free.
If you don't try to use me, I'll do you no harm,
So don't let him lock me in his house down in Carne.

Chorus

Written by Mick Hanly with additional lyrics by myself and Johnny Moynihan. It was performed on the anti-nuclear roadshow of 1978.

I see a dark cloud rising outside Wexford town,
I see a hard rain on Ireland pouring down.
There'll be no time to shelter. Let's all make a stand.
O'Malley's plan we'll have to ban or he'll destroy this land.

Chorus
It's the workers are being used again,
The workers are being used again.

They want four nuclear stations; who knows how many more?
If we are to stop them, we must defend Carnsore,
So men and women of Ireland, it's time to show your hand.
The lessons of France and the USA must make us understand.

Chorus

Two thousand jobs are promised, believe that if you can.
O'Malley's boys with all their ploys, they canvassed around the land,
In Carnsore, Easkey or Kilrush the ESB would build —
Should one go wrong, despite their talk, thousands could be killed.

Chorus

We never see their faces, these multi-national czars.
Our lands they rape from cape to cape, our seas they fill with tars.
The Westinghouse industrialist confessed to bribery;
I wonder if our leaders from corruption will be free.

It was in 1968 Jack Lynch went back to Cork
To open Whiddy Island where a handful of men got work.
The multi-national oil tycoons, they all turned out in style;
Ten years later fifty French lay slaughtered in the oil.

Chorus

And when it comes to dumping waste, here's what they plan to do:
They'll bury it in South Armagh and down in Wicklow too,
A nuclear waste triangle right at your front door
With poison manufactured at Windscale and Carnsore.

Chorus

They've tested round the valleys where the Finn goes sparkling down
To join the Shrule at bonny Lifford town,
But if there's radioactive waste where the stream goes running by
As down the Foyle the waters boil, you'll know the reason why.

So gather round you people, the fight has just begun,
We fought before, we know the score; this fight must be won.
Remember we've the sun up there, waiting for to turn
The wind, the tide, the ocean wide; there's energy to burn.

Chorus

A cairn built by anti-nuclear protesters at Carnsore, 1978. Art O'Laoghaire

I wrote this song after visiting Brendan McFarlane in the H-Blocks prior to the hunger strikes. He asked me if I could write a song which perhaps could make the people of the twenty-six counties more aware of what the H-Blocks and the dirty protest were all about.

I'm ninety miles from Dublin town,
I'm in an H-Block cell.
To help you understand me plight
This story now I'll tell.
I'm on the blanket protest,
My efforts must not fail
For I'm joined by men and women
In the Kesh and Armagh jail.

It all began one morning
I was dragged to Castlereagh
And though it was three years ago
It seems like yesterday.
For three days kicked and beaten,
I then was forced to sign
Confessions that convicted me
Of crimes that were not mine.

Sentenced in a Diplock court
My protest it began.
I could not wear this prison gear,
I was a blanket man.
I'll not accept their status,
I'll not be criminalised,
That's the issue in the blocks
For which we give our lives.

Over there in London town
Oh how they'd laugh and sneer
If they could only make us wear
Their loathesome prison gear.
Prisoners of war is what we are
And that we must remain.
The blanket protest cannot end
Till status we regain.

I've been beaten round the romper room
Because I won't say 'Sir'.
I've been frogmarched down the landing
And dragged back by the hair.

I've suffered degradation,
Humility and pain.
Still the spirit does not falter,
British torture is in vain.

I've been held in scalding water
While me back with deck scrubs was tore.
I've been scratched and cut from head to foot
Then thrown out on the floor.
I've suffered mirror searches,
Been probed by drunken bears,
I've heard me comrades cry and scream,
Then utter useless prayers.

Now with the news that's coming in
Our protest must not fail
For now we're joined by thirty girls
In Armagh women's jail.
So pay attention Irishmen
And Irish women too
And show the free state rulers that
Their silence will not do.

Though it's ninety miles to Dublin town —
It seems so far away —
There's more attention to our plight
In the USA.
Now you've heard the story
Of this filthy living hell,
Remember ninety miles away
I'm still in me H-Block cell.

On the Blanket

Written by Mick Hanly with additional lyrics by myself. It was performed by Moving Hearts during the hunger strikes and was a very emotive song. When I recall the performances of this song in those days I realise I've never experienced anything quite like it since and I particularly remember singing it in Sligo the night Martin Hurson died.

The truth comes as hard as the cold rain
On your face in the heat of the storm
And the stories I'm hearing would shock
   you
To believe that such deeds can go on.

You can starve men and take all their
   clothing,
You can beat them up till they fall,
You can break up the bodies but never
   the spirit,
Of those on the blanket.

The truth must be told so I'll tell it.
It all began five years ago.
Ciaran Nugent refused to be branded
A criminal and to wear prison clothes.

They threw him in naked to H-Block
And spat out their filthy abuse
And they left him awake till the cold
   light of day
With only a blanket.

Chorus
England, your sins are not over,
The H-Block still stands in your name
And though many voices have cried out
   to you
It's still your shame.
If we stay silent we're guilty
While these men lie naked and cold
In H-Block tonight, remember the fight
Of those on the blanket.

For four years this man and his comrades
In shameful conditions did lie;
From Dublin indifference and silence,
From London contempt undisguised.

Though life to these men was so precious
A hunger strike protest began
To try to move the cold hearts of the
    tyrants who keep
Those on the blanket.

How angry the March winds were
    blowing
As prisoners of war made their call
With deals and false promises broken.
How many more young men must fall?

The people have raised up their voices,
The world cries for justice in vain
To end the cruel torture and victory to
    gain
For those on the blanket.

Chorus

To-night as I stand here in Sligo
My heart filled with sorrow and shame
In mourning for young Martin Hurson,
His body laid down in Tyrone.

This young man had so much to live for.
His dying must not be in vain.
As we stand here tonight, let's remember
    the fight
Of those on the blanket.

Chorus

I learnt this many years ago while on the English folk club circuit. The lyric was
written by Bill Caddick to a Tchaikovsky tune. It has become one of my standards
and is popular in all parts of Ireland from Ballydehob to Ballymena.

When midnight comes and people homeward tread
Seek now your blankets and your feather bed.
Home comes the rover, his journey is over.
Yield up the night time to old John O' Dreams.

Across the hill the sun has gone astray,
Tomorrow's cares are many dreams away.
The stars are flying, your candle's dying.
Yield up the night time to old John O' Dreams.

Both man and master in the night are one.
All things are equal when the day is done.
The prince and the ploughman, the slave and the freeman
All find their comfort in old John O' Dreams.

When sleep it comes the dreams come running clear.
The hawks of morning cannot reach you here.
Sleep is a river, flow on forever,
And for your boatman choose old John O' Dreams.

One day in 1983 I found myself with nothing to do so I took a little drive around Knock and what appeared before my eyes but a very, very long runway. I was so shocked by the situation that this song really wrote itself.

At the early age of thirty-eight
Me mother said, 'Go West!
Get up,' says she, 'and get a job.'
Says I, 'I'll do me best.'

I pulled on me Wellingtons
To march to Kiltimagh
But I took a wrong turn in Charlestown
And ended up in Knock.

Oh once this quiet crossroads
Was a place of gentle prayer
Where Catholics got indulgent
Once or twice a year.

You could buy a pair of rosary beads
Or get your candles blessed.
If you had a guilty conscience
You could get it off your chest.

Then came the priest from Partry,
Father Horan was his name,
And since he's been appointed
Knock has never been the same.

'Begod,' says Jem, ' 'tis eighty years
Since Mary was about.
'Tis time for another miracle.'
He blew the candle out.

Chorus
From Fatima to Bethlehem,
From Lourdes to Kiltimagh,
There's never been a miracle
Like the airport up in Knock.

To establish terra firma
He drew up a ten year plan
And started running dances
Around 1961.

He built a fantabalous church,
Go h-Álainn on the holy ground,
And once he had a focal point
He started to expand.

Chip shops and Bed and Breakfasts
Sprung up over night.
Once a place for quiet retreats
Now a holy sight.

All sorts of fancy restaurants
For every race and creed
Where black and white and yellow
      pilgrims
All could get a feed.

The stalls once under canvas
Became religious supermarts
With such a range o' godly goods,
They had top twenty charts.

While the airport opposition
Was destroyed by James' trump card.
For centenary celebrations
He got John Paul the twenty-third.

Chorus

'We had the Blessed virgin here,'
Bold Jamesie did declare,
'And Pope John Paul the twenty-third*
Appeared just over there.

'Now do you mean to tell me,'
He said in total shock,
'That I am not entitled
To an airport here in Knock.'

TD's were lobbied and harassed
With talk of promised votes
And people who'd been loyal for years
Now spoke of changing coats.

Eternal damnation was
Threatened on the flock
Who said it was abortive
Building airports up in Knock.

Now everyone is happy,
The miracle is complete.
Father Horan's got his runway;
It's eighteen thousand feet.

All sorts of planes could land there,
Of that there's little doubt,
Handy for the Yankees
To keep the Russians out.

Did NATO donate, me boys, did NATO
    donate the dough?
Did NATO donate, me girls, did NATO
    donate the dough?

*Balladic License

127

In memory of a man whom I admired for many years and who subsequently became a very good friend, the late Seamus Ennis. He always gave me great encouragement as a singer and taught me many fine songs. I spent many a happy hour listening to him talking about his life and music and about his collecting of music. I felt that he didn't receive the recognition he deserved for all the work he did down through the years for Irish culture; this song is my little tribute to him. The mobile home he lived in is called Easter Snow.

Chorus
Oh the Easter snow
It is faded away,
It was so rare and so beautiful,
Now it's melted back into the clay.

Those days will be remembered
Beyond out in the Naul,
Listening to the master's notes
As gently they did fall.
Oh. . . .the music
As Seamus he did play,
But the thaw crept over the mantle white
And turned it back to clay.

Chorus

He gazed at the embers in reflection,
He called up lost verses again,
He smiled at a roguish recollection,
While his fingers gripped the glass to
    stem the pain.
When knocked on, his door would
    always open
With a welcome he'd bid the time of day.
Though we came when the last flakes
    were melted
While it lay upon the ground we stayed
    away.

Chorus

Seamus Ennis leaving the stage after final gig, Lisdoonvarna 1983. Colm Henry

I sometimes find myself in a situation which requires a song; usually this will be suitable for one performance only. The Literary and Historical Society in University College Dublin is the launching pad for many an illustrious reactionary career — the annually changing leader of this society is known as its auditor. On 25 November 1982 I performed a concert in Theatre L of UCD. Next door in Theatre M a debate was taking place from which Danny Morrison, the elected representative from Tyrone, was excluded. I performed this song on that evening.

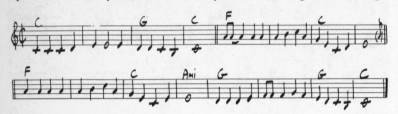

Justice Thomas Higgins is a man you all should know.
Sitting in the Specials he runs a nasty show,
Dispersing Irish justice in a way that makes me rage,
And once he was the auditor of the college L & H.

Mr Patrick Connolly is a man of great renown.
Recently he was the talk of every pub in town.
As attorney general thought it wise to disengage,
And once he was the auditor of the college L & H.

Patrick snide smug Cosgrave is Maggie Thatcher's right-hand man.
In a national university his illusions they began.
To mould her vicious strategy he joined the entourage,
And once he was the auditor of the college L & H.

This year's young incumbent was barely off the train.
Seeking power and prejudice he joined young Fine Gael.
To be like Higgins, Connolly, Cosgrave, Cormac Lacey craved,
And he is this year's auditor of the college L & H.

To celebrate elections his first debate he planned
To feature Conor Cruise O'Brien, a once respected man,
A Unionist called Millar and also Liam de Paor.
With the Tyrone people's mandate, Danny Morrison was there.

Cruiser and the Loyalist, they did collaborate.
Free speech for Republicans they could not tolerate.
Morrison was banished, Cormac Lacey sealed his fate.
That's why he's the auditor of the college L & H.

Or 'The Man from RTE'. Written by Fintan Valley to commemorate the visit of the 'Today Tonight' team from RTE to the small town of Ballinamore in Co. Leitrim.

'Leitrim is a very funny place, sir, a strange and troubled land.
All the boys are in the IRA, sir, all the women in Cumann na mBan
Every tractor has a Nicky Kelly sticker, displayed for all to see.
Sure it was no wonder that the Gardai made a blunder,'
Sez your man from RTE.

Chorus

'Every bird, upon my word, is singing, "I'm a rebel," sir, up in Mohill sir,
Every hen indeed is laying hand grenades, I do declare, sir, in Dromahair, sir,
Every crock of a Leitrim cock is longin to be free.
Even sheep are advisin' there'll be another risin',
Sez your man from RTE.

'**Today Tonight** went to Ballinamore, sir, they were briefed by the Gardai.
On a video they showed to me the Provies 'atin curry and drinkin' tea,
They were all wearin' Russian balaclavas, each carried an RPG,
British scalps around the tummy, pockets full of stolen money,'
Sez your man from RTE.

Chorus

'Leitrim is seething with sedition, it's Sinn Fein through and through.
All the task force have joined the local unit, the post office is the GHQ.
They've a race track underground for training Shergar, "no commint" is all they say to me,
Subversion here is bubblin', oh please take me back to Dublin,'
Sez your man from RTE.

Chorus

Margaretta D'Arcy wrote this tribute to the prisoners; many ex-Armagh women have remarked upon the accuracy of its portrayal of the time and the place.

In Black Armagh of the Goddess Macha,
Last February in the grey cold jail,
The governor Scott in his savage fury
Came down to break the women's will.
'Forty jailers, my forty jailers,
From the hell of Long Kesh come down
And help me break these warrior women
Who will not yield to the power of the
  Crown.'

The forty jailers put on their armour,
Strapped on their helmets, took up their
  shields,
Then they beat the Armagh women, they
  beat them down,
They were sure they'd yield.
Three days he kept them locked up in
  darkness,
Locked up in filth you would not believe.
When he released them he was so
  conceited
That one and all he thought they would
  yield.

'If you have suffered,' he smilingly said,
'It never happened, it was all just a
  dream.
Come out, come out and obey my
  orders.'
But the Armagh women they would
  never yield.
They'd never yield to Scott the Governor,
They'd never yield till they broke him
  down.
He and his jailers were all locked in
  prison
By the women of Armagh jail.

And there they remain, those warrior
  women,
Locked up in filth you could not believe.
They hold Scott and his warders
  powerless.
They hold them there, they'll never
  concede.
Women of Ireland, stand up and declare.
Women of Ireland, understand your
  power.
Make us see that together we'll do it
We'll tumble down their stone grey
  tower.

In Black Armagh of the Goddess Macha
Last February in a cold grey cell. . .

Maureen Gibson, Rosie Nolan and Anne Bateson. Smuggled from inside Armagh Prison

The Swiss are always so perfect, clean and wholesome, exact, unerring and precise. One evening it all fell apart, and Jim Page was there.

Young people on the street they meet
Underneath the lamp light bright
Outside diamond jewellery windows
Dazzling their sight at night.
Anger in their blood it pounds,
Echoes in a hallow sound.
It all comes tumbling down
In Zurich.

What the children learn at school
Is all that glitters must be gold.
Those who don't accept this rule
Find themselves out in the cold,
Sent there by a well-to-do, beautiful
   people
Who don't have time for the likes of you
In Zurich.

It all began one morning fine
When the government money came to
   town.
A fortune went to the concert hall;
Not one penny trickled down
To the youth centre in the middle of
   town.
They want to close it down,
Don't want young people hanging round
In Zurich.

Suddenly a spark did light
Upon that well remembered night.
In a flash, with bricks and bottles,
Came a most surprising sight.
Fired by a smouldering heat.
Five thousand angry children meet
And break every window in that most
   beautiful street
In Zurich.

Anarchy and streets of gold,
Lights are flashing, sirens wail.
Frightened eyes behind the windows
Watch the children go to jail.
Soldiers in well-armed ranks
Behind water cannon tanks
With plastic bullets to protect the banks
Of Zurich.

How can such trouble be?
Is this the writing on the wall?
The pillars of society
Make a very anxious call.
Quietly they call for peace,
Discipline to say the least,
What we need is more police
In Zurich.

From the garden of Geneva
To the flowery streets of Amsterdam,
Inside the walls of West Berlin
Troubles go from hand to hand.
Children left in the cold
Bring anarchy to the streets of gold.
That's what I was told
In Zurich, Zu, Zu, Zu, Zu.

Written by John Maguire of Cork. Music by Karl Byrne and Tony Walsh.

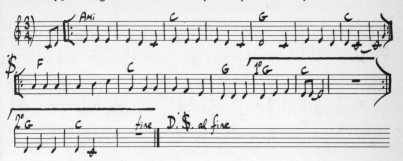

I remember the show twenty-one years ago
When John Kennedy paid us a visit;
Now the world's rearranged — not improved, only changed —
But our heart's in the same place — or is it?

Chorus
Hey Ronnie Reagan, I'm black and I'm pagan,
I'm gay and I'm left and I'm free
I'm a non-fundamentalist environmentalist,
Please don't bother me.

You're so cool, playing poker with death as the joker,
You've nerve but you don't reassure us
With those paranoid vistas of mad Sandinistas:
Are you really defending Honduras?
You'll be wearing the green down at Ballyporeen,
The town of the little potato;
Put your arms around Garret and dangle your carrot,
But you'll never get me to join NATO.

Chorus

Do you share my impression the world's in recession,
There's rather too much unemployment?
Still with Pershing and Cruise we'll have nothing to lose
But millions in missile deployment.
We can dig shelter holes when we've bartered our souls,
For security then we can shovel, while the myth of our dreams
Turns to nightmares, it seems:
From the White House straight back to the hovel.

Chorus

Since the Irish dimension has won your attention
I ask myself just what's your game:
Do your eyes share the tears of our last fifteen years
Or is that just a vote-catchers gleam?
Your dollars may beckon, but I think we should reckon
The cost of accepting your gold;
If we join your alliance, what price our defiance,
What's left if our freedom is sold?

Chorus

Written in London on 21 April 1984 for an anti-racist concert, promoted by the GLC at the Queen Elizabeth Hall. Dedicated to Ken Livingstone.

I first arrived in London back in 1963.
Though I've travelled ever since, it's still the place for me.
In Camden town and Cricklewood, I've got the curtain call
And once or twice I did a turn up in the Albert Hall.

Invited by the Council upon this royal stage,
To do an anti-racist gig, myself they did engage.
Since I have arrived here I'm very shocked to see
That Margaret and her boot-boys plan to sink the GLC.

Pavorotti sings in Finchley for Margaret and her crew,
James Galway plays for millionaires aboard the QE2,
Covent Garden caters for the fur coats and the whigs,
But the GLC will try and see that the unemployed have gigs.

Racing out in Goodwood and yachts in Maidenhead,
Boating down on Henley; all you need is bread.
Keep the fun all to themselves, that's what the Tories do,
But the GLC will try and see there's fun for me and you.

Denis Thatcher will become Lord Mayor, Mark Thatcher will set the rates,
Margaret Thatcher will become the Queen when the Queen she abdicates.
She'll have Cruise on Hyde Park Corner, plastic bullets in Southall,
The paras back from Crossmaglen to protect Whitehall.

As a humble Mick or Paddy on this royal stage,
I must admit to bias that I cannot disengage,
For Livingstone's the only one who could make the time
To enter into West Belfast and walk across the line.

Mick Tracy was big on the ballad scene in the late sixties and we had many the song together in 'The Castle' in the 'ballad boom' era. He returned to his native Mitchelstown to make cheese and recently sent me this song. Old singers never die, they only churn away.

I dreamt last night as I lay on my bed —
Where else can a poor boy dream —
That I was transported o'er mountain and
  hills
To the village of Ballyporeen.
I met Mr Reagan, that world famous
  actor.
Says he to me with a smile,
'Hey, Paddy, I'll give you some Pershing
  and Cruise
For to plant round the old Emerald Isle.

'If Ireland will join NATO, I'll look after
  yez all,
I'll build missile sites all over the land.
Give me one site and I promise in return
To bring Ian Paisley back to the Ku Klux
  Klan.
I'll build all my missiles of the finest Irish
  steel,
Assemble the lot down in Cork.
I'll build a six-lane highway from
  Castlerea to Templemore
And I'll finish off the airport up in Knock.'

'Hould on, Mr Reagan,' I made my reply,
'We don't want your artillery here.
You got your way with Helmut Schmidt,
Maggie Thatcher as well,
But you won't build a Greenham
  Common here.'

I wrote this in celebration of the news of Willy's arrival in Ireland in the summer of '84.

I just heard William Nelson: he was singin' of his hard life on the road
And his lyrics set me thinkin' it's much the same no matter where you go,
Be it Tulsk or Bord Na Móna, Arkansas or Arizona, the Liffeyside or the Shandon Bell;
I've received my education in the lounges of the nation; after twenty years I'm still goin'
    fairly well.

I've played every lounge in Ireland from Dingle right up to Donegal,
I've done 'Nancy Spain' on stages where no other ballad singers go at all,
From the Rising Sun in Brownstown to the Unyoke Inn just outside Wexford Town,
Ballymurphy and the Bogside, Ballinamore and even once in Ballinasloe.

Chorus
If I get an encore I go home feelin' like a king;
It's a two way situation: I get a lot of pleasure when I sing.

When I first heard Tommy Makem and the Clancys my future it was sealed,
I was bitten by the music bug and the wound it never healed.
When I got my first guitar my fingers bled until I learnt a chord or two;
I pulled on my Aran sweater, wrote me Ma a goodbye letter and started singin' in
    O'Donoghue's.

I was playin' in the Meeting Place when half the Special Branch came through the door;
They were lookin' for McGlinchey but they never found who they were lookin' for;
They started listenin' to my gig and hung around till after the show,
So if I ever need a taxi-plate or a massage at the special rate the Special Branch they told me
    where to go.

Chorus

Val, Christy and Juno at Carnsore, 1978. Derek Speirs (Report)

INDEX

Also published by

BRANDON

Falls Memories by Gerry Adams. Illustrated by
Michael McKernon.
"Especially valuable because it has been written by someone who has
strong and deep-rooted ties and involvement in both the class and
Republican struggles." — **Irish News**

Baulox by Tony Cafferky

"A brave new world of the late 20th century. For all its humour and funny
incidents, **Baulox** can be read as a serious warning to us all to hang on to
our humanity and sense of anarchy despite what They say." — **In Dublin**

Twist and Shout by Philip Davison

"Very alive and very funny, with a strong sense of irony. It's also very
relevant. Terry Hatchel and his friends are as much a part of Irish urban
culture today, with their casual attitude to drugs and sex and their
indifference to the Church and to the norms of middle class suburbia, as
Edna O'Brien's country girls were to the world of repressed sexuality and
drab conformity in the early 1960s." — **In Dublin**

An Irish Literary Quiz Book by Paddy Lysaght.

Illustrated by Tom Mathews.
"Delightful, tantalising and amusing. . . an ideal volume for a long train journey. At the end one knows a lot more about Irish literature." — **Irish Post**

Man of the Triple Name by John B. Keane

"Hugely enjoyable." — **In Dublin**
"Hilarious social history." — **Boston Irish News**

British Intelligence and Covert Action by Jonathan Bloch & Patrick Fitzgerald

The book Margaret Thatcher wants to ban, it "confirms the widely held view that the security services actually threaten our Freedom and Democracy" (Tony Benn, MP).

Green and Gold: The Wrenboys of Dingle by Steve MacDonogh

"Compulsive reading, a privileged peep through a Dingle keyhole. . . An excellent entertaining book." — **Books Ireland**

Fr McDyer of Glencolumbkille: An Autobiography

"A socialist, a radical, a Catholic priest, that strange combination which even Peadar O'Donnell found it difficult to understand." — **Fortnight**

The House by Leland Bardwell

A fine, haunting novel about love denied and love experienced, about "what a house and a family do to everyone, how lives are shaped and generations shoved into each other like the bellows of a concertina."

The Jimmy Ingle Story by Jimmy Ingle

Jimmy Ingle is one of Dublin's own; the first Irishman to win a European amateur boxing title, he was a hero when the city's working class had little to cheer about. With an introduction by Patrick Myler; illustrated.

For our full catalogue please write to
Brandon Book Publishers, Cooleen, Dingle, Co. Kerry, Ireland;

in the USA please write to
Brandon Book Publishers, 51 Washington Street,
Dover, New Hampshire 03820.